Neighborhoods of Cincinnati

Clifton

Clifton

Neighborhood and Community
in An Urban Setting
A Brief History

HENRY D. SHAPIRO & ZANE L. MILLER

COMMONWEALTH BOOK COMPANY
ST. MARTIN, OHIO

Copyright © 1976, by Henry D. Shapiro and Zane L. Miller
Copyright © 2014, by Commonwealth Book Company, Inc.

All rights reserved. No part of this book may be reproduced in any form or by any means without the prior written consent of the publisher, excepting brief quotes used in reviews. Printed in the United States of America.

Illustration Credits

The publisher thanks and credits the following: The Public Library of Cincinnati, Archives and Rare Books Library of the University of Cincinnati, Jean Sheblessy, Cincinnati History Library and Archives, Cincinnati Museum Center, Richard Wagner & Roy Wright, *Cincinnati Streetcars. No. 1, Horsecars and Steam Dummies* (Cincinnati, The Wagner Car Company, 1968), D. J. Kenny, *Illustrated Cincinnati* (Cincinnati, 1875), Daniel Drake, *Natural and Statistical View of Cincinnati* (Cincinnati, 1815), Henry Howe, *Howes Historical Collections* (1900).

Cover Photograph

Parkview Manor, completed in 1895 as a home for George B. Cox, became a famous Cincinnati landmark because Cox dominated Cincinnati politics from 1893 until 1913 and earned a national reputation as one of the nation's most efficient and venal big city political bosses. Samuel Hannaford, a prolific Cincinnati architect designed not only Parkview Manor but also Music Hall and City Hall, a choice of artists reflective of Cox's pronounced devotion to "boosting" the city's economic and cultural development. Cox died in 1916 of natural causes (a stroke), and the house remained in the Cox family until 1938. It served next (1938-1947) as a dormitory for Cincinnati Union Bethel, a social service agency that provided refuge and rehablitation facilities and other services for young and adult women. In 1947 it became the fraternity house for Pi Kappa Alpha. One of its members, Michael Dever, purchased the property in 2007, and three years later donated it to the Public Library of Cincinnati and Hamilton County for use as a new Clifton branch facility. Devers' generous civic gesture earned him the gratitude of living Cliftonites, and it probably also pleased Cox. Relentlessly depicted by good government advocates as a disgrace to the city of Cincinnati and the Clifton community—a man, they contended, who epitomized political corruption and made Cincinnati the worst governed city in the country—Cox insisted, as he put it, that a boss was "not necessarily a public enemy," an assertion subsequently taken seriously by historians. *Parkview Manor* stands as the last physical memorial to Cox, whose admirers built in the 1920s the Cox Theater (right next door to the Shubert) in downtown Cincinnati, an edifice (like the Shubert) the city of Cincinnati demolished in the 1970s as part of its central business district rehabilitation campaign.

Zane L. Miller, 2014

The Neighborhoods of Cincinnati Series

The *Neighborhoods of Cincinnati* series explores the rich and diverse cultural life of the city's basic building blocks. Cincinnati began its existence in the late eighteenth century as a spearhead of the urban frontier and as a gateway to a vast inland empire, America's Empire of Liberty, as Thomas Jefferson and his fellow founders of the Republic thought of it. Under that regime Cincinnati flourished, and by 1850 ranked as the Queen City of the West, the sixth largest city in the United States, first among cities west of the Appalachian Mountains, and sixth in the nation in manufacturing. Such a dynamic place attracted and continued to attract a multi-cultural agglomeration of native and foreign born people, who settled the place neighborhood by neighborhood and established an astonishing array of civic, social, economic, and artistic organizations. The proliferation of these neighborhoods, communities, and institutions spilled over into Northern Kentucky, crept easterly and westerly along the Ohio River, and edged up what are now the I-75 and I-71 expressway corridors toward Dayton and Columbus. The series will explore these entities and their role in creating the texture and patterns of urban life in Cincinnati's metropolitan region, one of the largest and most vibrant in a nation of competing cosmopolitan areas, and in the process compose chapters in the history of the American urban sweepstakes.

The series is organized and edited by Zane L. Miller, Charles Phelps Taft Professor Emeritus of History, University of Cincinnati, and co-editor of The Urban Life, Landscape, and Policy Series, Temple University Press, and by Charles F. Casey-Leininger, Associate Professor of History, University of Cincinnati, and Director of the Department of History's Public History Program.

Zane L. Miller
Charles F. Casey-Leininger

Editor's Introduction

Two sets of interests converged in this slim volume. The first was that of Henry D. Shapiro and Zane L. Miller who sought to train university students in how to learn history by doing it, a concept then, as now, more often wished for than practiced. The second involved some residents of Cincinnati's Clifton neighborhood, who wanted to commemorate the history of their community on the occasion of the nation's bicentennial and the neighborhood's annual house tour for 1976. They approached Miller and Shapiro in 1975, who set to work and produced this brief history published in 1976. Shapiro wrote the introduction and the first seven parts, and Miller wrote the last three.

The authors already had accumulated some of the material for the book, because in 1973 they had established an undergraduate research seminar they named the Laboratory in American Civilization. Among the first projects Miller, Shapiro, and their students tackled was the question of how Clifton, an elite suburb of Cincinnati in the mid-nineteenth century, became, through annexation, a Cincinnati neighborhood by the end of the century, and then in the middle of the twentieth century, a part of the city whose community council, the Clifton Town Meeting, which the city authorized to participate in the planning of the neighborhood's future development.

Miller and Shapiro approached the teaching of the seminar from the point of view that students learn best by defining and solving manageable historical problems, guided by teachers who can provide resources and foster seminar discussions about how the resolution of one problem helps both to illuminate related issues and to define new problems for investigation. "We sought," Miller and Shapiro wrote, "...to create a laboratory situation in which the process of inquiry took place...through actual participation by students working as individuals, where the rewards of the process of inquiry...could be shared by all the students as a continuous process throughout the academic year." In this way, students in the seminar identified an array of problems and examined a variety of subjects. These included the role of the Ohio state legislature in regulating the incorporation of villages and cities, the changing rules for obtaining or resisting annexation, and the changing contents and categories in federal decennial census reports, including census takers' manuscript head counts on the populations of villages and cities.

The seminar protocol made a distinction between local history as "particularist history" and local history as "symptomatic" history. Shapiro and Miller tried to persuade their students that local history was worth doing not only because of people's interest in a particular place, but also because, as the name of their seminar suggests, the history of a particular place could be seen as symptomatic of more general problems, issues, trends, and tendencies. Indeed, they argued that in this seminar, as in a scientific laboratory, the process of examining how Cliftonites defined and solved problems provided clues about how Americans in other places in the same time-period tried to order their lives. As Shapiro phrased it, the seminar's approach to doing "...local history is not merely antiquarianism," for it "provides an opportunity to look ... at phenomena which appear in larger and more unmanageable form in the history of the nation, and in human history more generally; and that to this degree, the history of Clifton, or indeed of any other place, is the history of American Civilization."

So in 1975, when some members of Clifton Town Meeting approached Miller about writing a pamphlet on the history of Clifton for their 1976 house tour, Shapiro and Miller had the material developed by the "Lab's" seminar participants. This provided them not only with information about the lovely old houses of the village's mid-nineteenth century elite, but also with some dimensions of the transformation of Clifton from an elite rural village several miles from Cincinnati to a modern neighborhood of that city. That made it possible for Shapiro and Miller to conduct additional research and create in a relatively short period of time a coherent story by fleshing out the stages of that transformation in concise and essentially chronologically arranged "chapters," each of which examined Clifton's past from the point of view of problem definition and resolution by its residents and sometimes by outsiders.

This brief history in its final segments expressed a concern about city planning and city governance in the mid-twentieth century that, Miller argues, remains an issue in the twenty-first century. By the 1970s, Clifton's civic leaders had concluded that Clifton should become an autonomous community with a right to self-determination and distinct character of its own. This longing for independence appeared in the 1975 Clifton Community Plan prepared by the Clifton's neighborhood organization with the assistance of the Cincinnati Planning Department. The plan both projected a misleading image of Clifton as a "bucolic and isolated 19th century village," while also picturing it as a diverse community determined to "retain in the Clifton environs, a variety of research and educational institutions, and to develop educational and recreational facilities cut in a sophisticated cosmopolitan, and decidedly contemporary mold." This contradiction between the insular and the cosmopolitan, Miller contended, arose from the inability of Cliftonites, in their quest for self-determination, to develop a clear conception of an interdependent relationship between all the "suburbs, neighborhoods, and communities" of the city and its metropolitan area, a problem characteristic of civic and political leaders in other Cincinnati neighborhoods and suburban municipalities.

Miller subsequently expanded on his and Shapiro's discussion of Clifton and it's problems as symptomatic history in *Visions of Place: The City, Neighborhoods, Suburbs, and Cincinnati's Clifton, 1850-2000*, in which he extended the story forward to the last decades of the twentieth century. This book concluded with the expression once again of reservations about the temptations of neighborhood autonomy and insularity. Such a vision, Miller noted, had appeared in the Clifton Neighborhood Plan of 1975, and again in 1992, when the Clifton Town Meeting installed signs (still there) near the boundaries of the old Clifton village that said, "Welcome to Clifton, Incorporated 1850." These signs, wrote Miller, "reinforced the idea of neighborhood autonomy and dissociated" the neighborhood organization from any "concept of the public interest that embraced a local entity larger than Clifton." Miller also contended that the problems arising from neighborhood autonomy raise "serious questions about the wisdom and utility of planning neighborhood by neighborhood without reference to the welfare of the whole [city] and [the] antigovernment animus that drives the quest for neighborhood autonomy. It points particularly," he asserted, "to the importance of retrieving the idea of the public interest defined as the welfare of the whole" as a strategy for treating the persistence of racial residential segregation and other unresolved urban problems.

We cannot tell how that will turn out, but Miller in the brief Clifton history addressed the matter in an optimistic mood. Cliftonites in the 1970s, he indicated, "seemed tempted ...to turn inward...,to assume that Clifton somehow could take care of itself, and to forget its potential role as a dynamic place ... in ... the city and metropolis of which it formed a part....Yet to their great credit...they did not act decisively on that turning inward impulse ." And, Miller observed in 2014, most Cliftonites seldom acted consistently on these uncompromisingly isolationist urges. Instead, like their predecessors in the post-annexationist years, they seem to have accepted and made the best of the delights, dilemmas, and drawbacks of their dual allegiance to neighborhood and city, and to city and nation.

This brief history of Clifton is an early example of work that originated from teaching methods and analytical concepts that served as the basis for the Laboratory in American Civilization. Other examples may be found in a number of theses, dissertation, articles, essays, and books by students who worked with Shapiro and Miller. Indeed, they used to refer jokingly to themselves and the authors of these works as practitioners of the "Cincinnati school" of urban history. The school's members include Alan Marcus, who wrote the essay on Henry Shapiro in the appendix of this booklet, and the author of this introduction.

Charles F. Casey-Leininger
University of Cincinnati
November, 2014

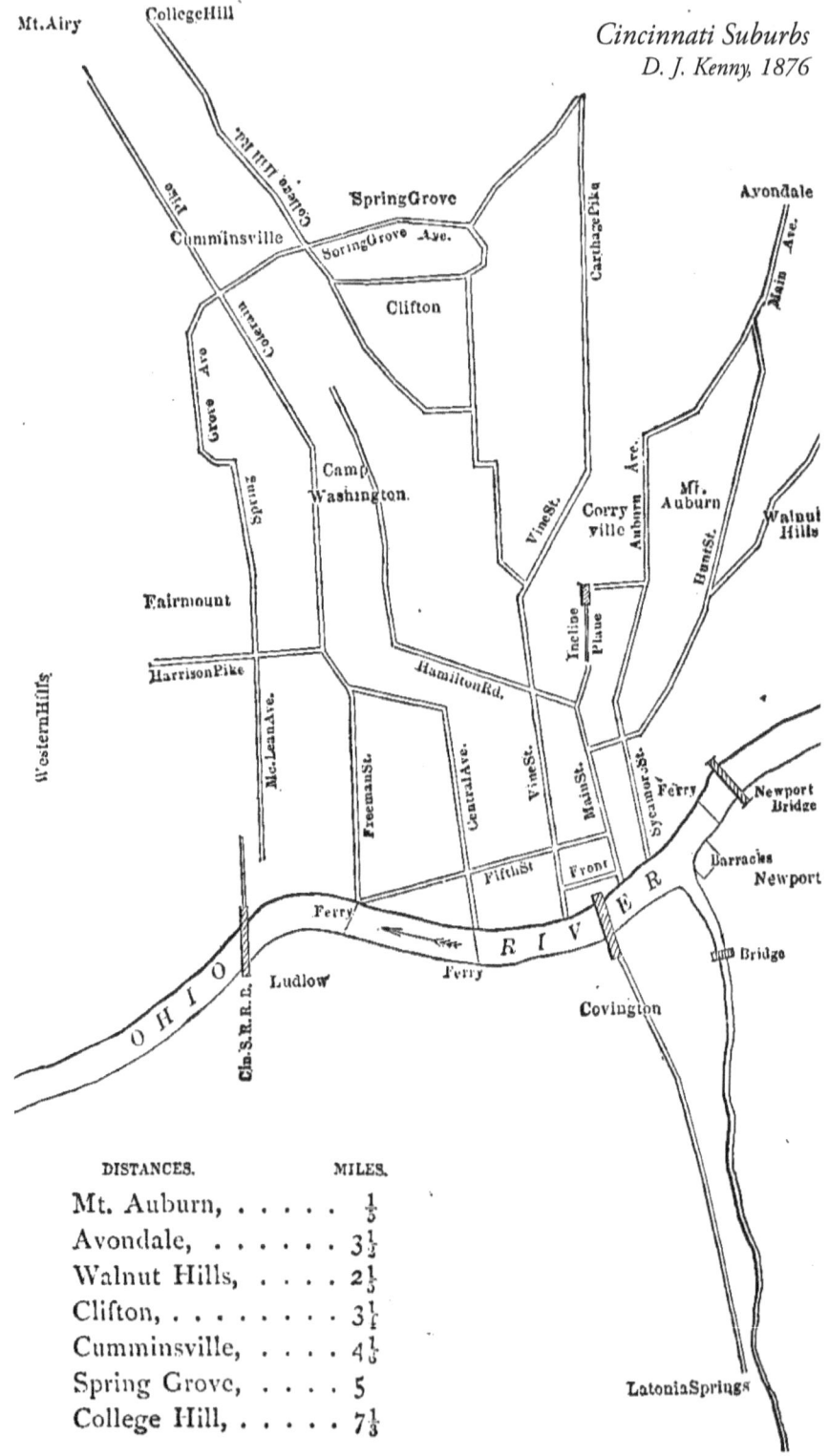

Table of Contents

Acknowledgments • *xiii*

Introduction • *xv*

The Beginnings of Clifton • *1*

The Settlement of the Country • *10*

Incorporation and its Consequences: • *21*
The Emergence of a Suburb

Clifton School and a Sense of Place • *26*

Annexation and the Idea of Suburb • *33*

The New Clifton and its Stately Homes • *41*

The Short Road to Neighborhood • *50*

Clifton as Neighborhood: • *52*
The Post Annexation Years

Neighborhood and City • *60*

Neighborhood as City: • *68*
The Rise of the Community
Idea in Clifton

Further Reading • *75*

About the Authors • *77*

Acknowledgments

The occasion for the preparation of this brief history is the 1976 House Tour sponsored by the Clifton Town Meeting, but its origins lay in the establishment of the Laboratory in American Civilization at the University of Cincinnati, and our attempt there to begin a systematic examination of local history as symptomatic history. From the work of the Laboratory has come our growing sense of the appropriateness of the task we set for ourselves in 1973, as well as much of our understanding of both the history of Clifton and of the relationship of Clifton to the larger city of which it is a part. We wish therefore to acknowledge at the outset our deep debt to our students, who asked the right questions and forced us to clarify our own notions about history in general and the history of Cincinnati more particularly, and who did much of the preliminary research upon which this study is based. In particular, we must thank for their efforts Betsy Schwartz, Christopher Noell, Tracy Thomas, Patricia Tighe, Mark Winfield, Carl Gruenenger, Gail Jordan, Michael Nauer, Missi Meyer, and Amy Peters, who appeared at the last-minute to help resolve persisting difficulties in the details of Clifton's history.

This history of Clifton, like all others, is built upon the pioneering efforts in local history of Dr. Arthur King, whose splendid articles in the *Bulletin of the Cincinnati Historical Society* have made available a wealth of information, especially about the early history of our community. It is a pleasure to thank him publicly, as we all have thanked him privately, for these important contributions to scholarship.

In preparing this history for publication, we have worked closely with several members of the Clifton Town Meeting, and wish to acknowledge our debt for support and encouragement, particularly to Shirley Richfield, who was the driving force behind the project; Harriet Van Ginkel, who provided us with much information about the older homes of Clifton; and Jean Sheblessy, who provided us with photographs of the homes on the 1976 House Tour. Dottie Lewis, Laura Chace, and the staff of the Cincinnati Historical Society assisted us in the location of the older photographs reproduced herein, and made the Society's rich collections of library and manuscript materials available for our use and for the use of our students. Helen Slotkin, Alice Vestal, and their colleagues in the Special Collections Department of the University of Cincinnati Library and its Metropolitan Studies Collection have been of enormous help throughout; without them, this study could not have been begun.

Funds in aid of publication have been provided by the University of Cincinnati, through its University Education Council and its Office of University Publications, as well as by the following members of the Clifton business community: the Central Trust Company; the Fidelity Federal Savings and Loan Association; the First National Bank; the Home Federal Savings and Loan Association; Jane Druffel, Cline Realtors; Louise Fletemeyer, Clifton Realtor; J.. Gilbert Geary, Theodore Mayer & Bros., Realtors; Stephen Gerdsen, West Shell, Inc.; Kathleen Martin, Shelton Realty Co.; William Parchman, Parchman & Oyler Realtors; Walter Sambi, Walter Sambi Realtor; Lance's Gift Shop. For their generous contribution of this most practical kind of assistance we are particularly grateful.

CINCINNATI *in 1810*

Introduction

In recent years, the newspapers and sometimes the politicians of Cincinnati have defined Clifton as that extended hilltop area north of McMillan Street and south of Mitchell Avenue, between Vine Street on the east and the Mill Creek expressway on the west. On the ridge are high rise apartment buildings and hundred year old mansions on many-acred landscaped lots, single family homes and multiple-unit dwellings, shops and restaurants, fast-food franchises and gas stations, banks and bars, and a cluster of charitable institutions which serve the entire city, and in some cases the nation, but which serve in any case as the principal employers in the neighborhood—the University of Cincinnati and the Hebrew Union College, the Deaconess and Good Samaritan Hospitals, the Bethesda Home and Hospital, the Cincinnati Crematorium, Hughes High and Clifton Elementary Schools. Add Burnet Woods Park and the two cemeteries, on the Vine Street hill north of Woolper and on Ludlow Avenue across from the intersection of Morrison, and Clifton appears as a complete and self-sufficient community, a place to be born, live, work, grow old, die, and be buried,

Clifton is a place to be born, live, grow old, die, and be buried, but by and large it is not a place to work, for Clifton's southern boundary in fact is not McMillan Street but Ludlow-Jefferson Avenue north of Burnet Woods on the east side of Clifton Avenue, and Dixmyth on the west side of Clifton Avenue. Deaconess and Good Sam, U.C. and H.U.C., Hughes High School and the Crematorium are outside of Clifton. So of course is Burnet Woods itself, except perhaps for its northwest corner which Anne Marshall donated to the city, and where Cliftonites maintain an evergreen tree decorated each year at Christmas-time by the Scouts. Clifton is thus dependent upon Cincinnati for employment and for much of its shopping (despite the recent vitality demonstrated by the Clifton-Ludlow business community), even as it depends upon Cincinnati for public services. And so it has always been.

The newspaper definition of Clifton as comprising the entire ridge, is the product of an essential urban consciousness, but Clifton itself was the creation of an essential suburban consciousness. It is that consciousness, and its consequences for the history of Clifton as a community, which is the real subject of this study.

This newspaper definition of Clifton, however incorrect it may be, makes sense, of course, and it is this quality of "sounding right" which explains its persistence. Clifton thus defined has the characteristics of a modern "neighborhood." It is bounded by major traffic arteries. More important, in the Clifton-Ludlow business strip it appears to have a "center." Clifton may thus be understood as just another of those numerous crossroads towns once outside of Cincinnati which the city annexed during the nineteenth century and thereby transformed into neighborhoods, each with its residual central-business-district, its mixed housing patterns, its concentric circles of land-use zones. Exurbanites in Finneytown or Indian Hill see no analogies between their own communities and Clifton, which because of its density and its age and its complex population mix appears to be part of the "inner"—by which we mean in part "older" city.

Clifton in fact did not develop as a crossroads town. It was never a self-sufficient place, as crossroads towns tend to be. It never aspired to be a city, to have a mixed economy, to be socially or politically independent of the city which lay three miles to the south. It did aspire to be a community. It depended for its definition on the existence of major traffic arteries which went around it, rather than through it, and from the mid-19th century it resisted, as it has continued to resist, the construction of more "modern" roads which would tie it more closely to other communities and which threatened to divide it against itself. Its hope was always that the city would pass it by, that it would be allowed to remain a separate place. But it sought to remain a special kind of place. What kind of place is the focus of this brief history.

In trying to find out, however, we hope to do other work as well. We hope to suggest that history is the story of people doing things and solving problems, that where they do things as well as how they do things are both part of the story even as where to do things, including where to live, is part of the problem to be solved. In the process, we hope also to suggest that "urban history" is as varied as the places people live and work, and that it thus includes "suburban" history; that local history is not merely antiquarianism but provides an opportunity to look "as under a glass and in an hour" at phenomena which appear in larger and more unmanageable form in the history of the nation, and in human history more generally; and that to this degree, the history of Clifton, or indeed of any other place, is the history of American Civilization.

The Beginnings of Clifton

Historic Clifton as defined by its charter of incorporation in 1850 consisted of "so much of the township of Mill creek, in the county of Hamilton, as is comprised within the following boundaries, to wit: so much of sections 22, 21, 15, and of the south half of 16, in the third township and second fractional range of townships of the Miami Purchase, as lie south and east of the Miami Canal, and west of the center of the Cincinnati and Carthage Turnpike road." The Miami Canal ran roughly along the route of Central Parkway to Ludlow Avenue. North and east of Ludlow, remains of its stone sides may still be seen, where it ran parallel to the Mill Creek south of Spring Grove Avenue. The Cincinnati and Carthage Turnpike, once maintained by the County, is now called Vine Street north of Glenmary, and Ruther between Glenmary and Jefferson. The southern border of sections 21 and 15 runs east and west along Howell Avenue, cuts off the northwestern corner of Burnet Woods Park, and continues east along a line some yards south of Wentworth, leaving the Cox mansion and the houses fronting on Jefferson Avenue east of Brookline, and the largest part of Burnet Woods, in section 14.

Both the historic boundaries of Clifton and its particular characteristics as a community were the results of historical accidents—who owned the land, how it was developed, and when. These in turn depended largely on the character of the land itself, what it was like and where it was located with reference to Cincinnati and to the transportation facilities which connected the city with its nineteenth century hinterland.

Some three miles northeast of old Cincinnati, Clifton was surrounded on three sides by valleys. Streams ran through the valleys, paths followed the streams and were widened and improved until they became roads. Where the valleys and the streams and the paths and the roads crossed each other the soil was usually rich and the location seemed convenient, and there came the people, whose settlements gave names to the roads which led to them. Ludlow Avenue was once the Cumminsville Turnpike and before that, the road to Ludlow's Station. Ruther Avenue was once the Hill Farm Road before it became part of the Carthage Turnpike, before it became Vine Street. Clifton Avenue north of Ludlow Avenue was Irwin's Mill Road until 1850, after

William Irwin who once owned a mill near the site of the old Winton Place Railroad Station, at the foot of the Clifton ridge to the north. And Clifton Avenue itself took its name from the road which ran north from McMillan Street, at the northernmost limit of the city of Cincinnati, one mile along the ridge to the Village of Clifton.

That was later, however, when there was a Village of Clifton. Before 1850 there was no Village. Before 1830, there were almost no people. Clifton was some 1200 acres of wooded hillside. The soil was clay with a thin covering of topsoil, of considerably less interest either to farmers or land speculators—who valued land by its potential for future sale—than the extensive acreage along the Mill Creek where the valley widened out south of Knowlton's Corners, or the valley land and the easier slopes northeast of the Mill Creek in Cumminsville and Winton Terrace, including the land now occupied by the Spring Grove Cemetery. Even after the Miami Canal opened in 1827, providing a convenient means of transporting agricultural products to the north and ultimately to the east coast, farms hugged the sides of the Clifton ridge, along the route of the Canal. From the top of the hill it was a long way down, and a longer way up. It was only with the coming of the horse-drawn omnibus and especially with the completion of the Cincinnati, Hamilton, and Dayton Railroad in 1851, which offered genuinely rapid transit from Winton Place or Knowlton's Corners into the city, that Clifton came to seem a desirable location, not for farms, however, but for many storied mansions.

For commuters, the very conditions which had limited the value of Clifton real estate for agricultural purposes meant that the same land could be had at reasonable prices for the establishment of "farms," "parks," or "estates," on which could be built summer homes or later, permanent dwellings. So soon as Americans discovered the romantic possibilities of landscape and scenic views, and so soon as the residents of Cincinnati amassed enough wealth to send an elite to the hilltops surrounding the city, Clifton came into its own. And the views must have been magnificent. The native trees were cut over in good 19th century fashion so that trees across the valleys might be seen, and so that, at least after 1851, residents might catch a glimpse of the passing railroad trains which were widely held to provide "interest" to the scene. Our taste in some things has changed, but even now, in winter when the Clifton trees are bare, one can walk the streets and imagine what it must have been like when in every direction one saw wooded hills, summer and winter. Go up in your imagination thirty feet to the tops of Clifton's older homes and one can see forever.

The land of Clifton, like all the other land lying between the Little and the Great Miami Rivers north of the Ohio, was first owned by John Cleves Symmes and his colleagues, as "proprietors" of the 333,000 acre Miami Purchase, acquired from the United States government in 1788. Like the Proprietors of New York, New Jersey, Delaware, or Pennsylvania in the 17th century or the Proprietors of South Carolina in the 18th century, like the directors of the "corporations" which settled Massachusetts Bay and Virginia, Symmes and his colleagues controlled the land but did not quite own it. The Company of Proprietors owned it. Individuals among this group could purchase land in fee simple, and individual Proprietors could reserve sections for future purchase. The Proprietors were to survey the land as required by the Ordinance of 1785, see to the establishment of local government as required by the Ordinance of 1787, and otherwise to act as the agents of the United States in distributing the land through sale to individual owners. In return, the Company of Proprietors received whatever profit accrued from the sale of land, and individual Proprietors purchasing or reserving land received whatever profit would come from the future sale of their own parcels, as the growth of population made lands in the Miami territory more valuable.

As required by the Ordinance of 1785, survey had to precede sale or reservation, and survey had to divide the land into equal, rectilinear, segments. The "ranges" were strips six miles wide running north and south. Townships were cut out of the ranges, each six miles square, and the townships in turn were subdivided into "sections"—36 in each township—each one mile square, containing 640 acres. The sections in each township were to be numbered consecutively from south to north and from east to west, so that sections 1-6 were in the easternmost row, 7-12 next to the west, and so on.

Mill Creek Township, in which Clifton is located, had its southern border at a line drawn from an imaginary point a little more than a mile south of the intersection of William Howard Taft Road and McMillan Street in east Walnut Hills, six miles due west to the intersection of Academy and Gurley in Price Hill. Its western border ran from this point due north to the middle of the Providence Hospital grounds. Its northern border ran east to the intersection of Section Road—the name persists—and Eastlawn and thence south to the point of beginning in the suburbs of Dayton, Kentucky across the river. The city of Cincinnati itself ended at the line where the Mill Creek Township began, along which a road later known as Liberty Street ran. The original survey lines thus created a legal barrier to the expansion of the city into contiguous territory, at least until the mid-century, after which annexation across township lines began.

Within the Miami Purchase itself, survey was not systematic nor settlement orderly. Lands were surveyed as need, and the availability of purchasers required. Settlement took place at random. This indeed was what made the Miami Purchase a viable investment, Symmes insisted. Unlike the Ohio Company lands around Marietta, where the "New England plan of connected towns or villages" was enforced by the Proprietors, and where settlement proceeded slowly as a result, Symmes said, "the different method for settling Miami puts it in the power of every purchaser to chuse his ground, and convert the same into a station, village or town at pleasure; and nothing controuls him but the fear of Indians. Therefore whenever ten or twelve men will agree to form a station, it is certainly done. This desultory way of settleing will soon carry many through the Purchase, if the savages do not frustrate them. Encouragements are given at every man's will to settlers, and they bid on each other in order to make their own post the more secure."

Among the first of the settlements thus made, in 1789 or 1790, was Ludlow's Station, now Cumminsville, where the Mill Creek Valley splits, to the northeast along Spring Grove Avenue, to the north along Hamilton Avenue, to the northwest along Colerain Avenue. It was one of a number of settlements promoted by Israel Ludlow, Symmes' chief surveyor, who laid claim in his own name to much of the best land not already reserved by the Proprietors, and joined with individuals among the Company of Proprietors, most notably Jonathan Dayton, in establishing such "stations, towns and villages" as the one which became Dayton, Ohio. It was Ludlow's Station in the Mill Creek, however, which provided the portal of entry for those who eventually came to settle the Clifton ridge and later, grown up into a town which bore Cummins' name instead, provided Clifton's commuting families access to the city where they worked and the shops where they shopped.

When he could, Ludlow purchased valley land exclusively, and left the hillsides and the hilltops to less discriminating speculators. So he purchased section 22 and got a little hillside land in the bargain, and he purchased section 27 in the valley west of Clifton, but left sections 21 and 15 alone. Section 16, northeast of the intersection of Clifton and Lafayette, might have met his specifications for investment property but was reserved for the support of schools, and hence not available. But so it was that most of section 21 came into the hands of John Symmes' sons-in-law, perhaps as wedding gifts. The northern half, from McAlpin to Lafayette Avenue at Clifton, belonged to Peyton Short. The southern half, from McAlpin to Howell, belonged to William Henry Harrison, who sold the more accessible and more valuable western half to Isaac Bates in 1803. And so it was also that the rougher land in section 15 was passed off to Silas Condict, one of Symmes' associates who remained in New Jersey and didn't know any better.

Land was land, however, Symmes and his generation traded land like baseball cards. Even if it were located on a hillside or at the top of a ridge, it had potential value. As population flooded the Ohio Valley on both sides of the river, a booming market developed, not only for farm land located near established centers of civilization, served by roads and protected by militia or continental troops, but also for less accessible acres of interest to speculators.

JOHN CLEVES SYMMES *(1742-1814) served as an officer in the Revolutionary War and represented New Jersey in the Continental Congress. In 1788 he moved with his family to southwestern Ohio to oversee the organization, survey, sale, and distribution of lands from the Miami Purchase, a 333,000 acre parcel acquired from Congress for $.67 per acre.*

ISRAEL LUDLOW *(1765-1804) came to Ohio as a young surveyor and helped complete the Seven Ranges survey, the first to be laid out according to the provisions of the Northwest Ordinance. In 1788 he joined the group establishing Cincinnati and he completed the town survey in 1789. He later laid out the towns of Hamilton and Dayton and, by the time of his death, likely had surveyed more of Ohio than any other surveyor.*

Because the Treaty of Greenville (1795) at once opened up the interior of Ohio but blocked migration to the northwest, Cincinnati and the Miami Valley towns became funnels through which population moved south and west along the river into southern Indiana and then, after Harrison had forced the Kaskaskia to cede the Illinois territory to the United States in 1803, further west to the plains.

So it was that Clifton land changed hands again and again during the 1790s and first years of the new century, sometimes by sale and sometimes by exchange, but always as part of the larger pattern of land speculation in the Miami Purchase and the Ohio Valley more generally. By 1803, however, the era of the first speculators had ended. The admission of Ohio to the union as a first state carved out of the Northwest Territory and the simultaneous opening of the Illinois lands to the west meant the emergence of Cincinnati and the Miami Valley as distinct places with distinct political and economic interests, and a future already taking shape, distinct from that of other areas in Ohio or in the west. At the same time, the complex and often chaotic economic entity which was the Miami Purchase began to tumble down as disputes over land titles, political conflict, and the bankruptcy of Symmes himself made vast territories available to local speculators as well as potential residents. Between 1803 and 1814 in any case, the outlines of the Clifton that was to be began to take shape beneath the hands of a second generation of local land owners and speculators.

It was during these years, for example, that William Irwin, a prominent Cincinnati merchant, acquired the northern half of section 21 from his daughter's father-in-law's brother-in-law, Peyton Short (Irwin's daughter married Harrison's son; Harrison and Short each married daughters of John Cleves Symmes), and the southeastern corner of section 22 from Israel Ludlow's extraordinary son, James. In 1814, Nicholas Longworth, who had acquired most of section 15 about 1809, sold off the last of his land across the Vine Street valley and, by improving the path which ran west of the stream through that valley, firmly defined the eastern limit of his 328 acre holding, and of Clifton itself. In that year also the southwestern quarter-section of section 21, acquired by Isaac Bates in 1803, was sold to Captain Andrew Mack, who was putting together an extensive farm in the Mill Creek Valley, except for 57 acres retained by Bates between what is now Morrison and the Canal. About 1814 also, Jesse Hunt, who had bought land in section 15 with or from Longworth around 1809, also acquired Harrison's remaining quarter section in section 21, between Morrison and Clifton, from Howell north to McAlpin.

Who lived in the Clifton area at this time, is not certain, although it seems clear that none of the owners did. Longworth at least was well known for renting or leasing agricultural land to tenants all over the county, and we may presume that much of his hillside land in section 15 was not allowed to lie fallow, but was in orchards if not grain and vegetables. And what Longworth did, others must have done also, for there is evidence that by 1827, when the Miami Canal was completed, Clifton area farmers shipped produce out of the valley. The mill-master and the workers at Irwin's Mill must also have lived nearby, but until historical archaeology combines with economic and legal history to explore this early period, the social character of Clifton must remain unknown. (It is tempting to wonder if Longworth's well-known proclivity for settling Europeans skilled in viticulture on his Cincinnati holdings manifested itself here in this early period, and if "Vine" street was not the original name only later resurrected when control of the Carthage Pike passed to the city.)

Land ownership and presumptive land use patterns in the Clifton area remained relatively unchanged for about a decade after 1814. The return of prosperity following the panic of 1819, manifested and then spurred by the decision of the Ohio Legislature to charter and support with public credit companies willing to construct canals in the State, by Act of 1825, however, yielded an almost modern pattern of land sale and land subdivision. No direct evidence of relationship between the opening of the Miami Canal in 1827 and the increase in the value of Clifton real estate can be found, in this period, but the general prosperity of Cincinnati during these years will surely have extended well beyond the city's limits. At the same time, and more immediately significant, the apparent bankruptcy of Andrew Mack in 1825, and the death of William Irwin in 1826, worked to place well over 500 acres—almost half of what is now Clifton—on the market within a year.

At about this time, moreover, land use patterns on either side of Clifton Avenue began to diverge. Section 21, to the west, remained an area of large lots, although ownership changed hands again and sometimes again. In 1825, for example, when Mack lost all of his "farm" to the Cincinnati Branch, Bank of the United States, the Bank did not subdivide but kept his 103 acres intact, and it was acquired in 1831 by Charles Clarkson, who was putting together a "farm" of his own. In the same way, Irwin's property, comprising the northern half-section in section 21 and the southeastern corner of section 22, although divided along the section line by his executors following his death in 1826, passed into the hands of Nicholas Longworth between 1830 and 1834. Longworth sold both parcels to Clarkson sometime before 1839. Only the southeastern quarter-section of section 21, once owned by William Henry Harrison, was divided during this period, into distinct parcels. The upper 60 acres were acquired by Elijah Wood in 1827. The lower 100 acres were sold to Henry Gregory in 1823, who in turn sold to Nicholas Longworth in 1833, who in turn sold to James Bryant that same year.

Longworth, who thus made a first appearance as broker and facilitator in transfers of section 21 property, during these same years functioned both as broker and as primary seller in a series of transactions which divided section 15 into a series of strips, plots and lots, some of which appear to have been rented or leased, and some of which were sold. One parcel, of 60 acres at the south end of section 15 west of Ruther, Longworth sold to Thomas Roberts in 1818, bought back at a sheriff's sale in 1826, and subsequently sold to Michael P. Cassily as part of the "Hill Farm" which he was putting together after 1830, as an investment, and which Cassily eventually gave to his daughter as dowry at the time of her marriage in 1839. Anne Marshall thus became the owner of a large parcel composed of smaller parcels, comprising all the land south of the houses off Interwood.

Just south of the point at which McAlpin meets Clifton was a 12 acre strip running east to Vine Street which Longworth first rented to William Montgomery, about 1818, and subsequently sold. Later subdivided, the six acres fronting on Clifton Avenue became the property of Gazzam Gano. North of this, a parcel of about 20 acres was sold to Jesse Miles, and eventually became the property of William Resor, who sold the 13 acre strip south of Woolper to a Mr. Doudle during the 1850s and the hilly land on either side of Juergens to a number of different owners, and built his grand summer home, "Greendale" in the middle of the original property, where Greendale Avenue now runs.

Half of Longworth's remaining property, north of the Miles-Resor land, was purchased by Aaron Ireland about 1826. Ireland lost it at a sheriff's sale in 1843, when it was bought by John Avery who turned around and sold 22 acres at the south end of the parcel to Flamen Ball, who held the mortgage on the whole, and the remaining 10 acres to Robert Buchanan. Longworth retained 33 acres at the crest of the Clifton ridge, and only sold them in 1843 to complete Buchanan's grand country estate, "Greenhills."

Nicholas Longworth (1783-1863) came to Ohio in 1804 and established a successful wine-making business, planting his vines on the hills overlooking the Queen City. So famous were his Catawba wines that Longfellow dedicated his "Ode to Catawba Wine" to Longworth, who became known as the "Father of American Grape Culture."

The Settlement of the Country

Despite these changes in land ownership, and the beginnings of subdivision in section 15, the character of Clifton during the 1820s and 1830s appears to have remained strikingly similar to the character of Clifton during the previous two decades. More of it may have been farmed, lots may have been slightly smaller on the east side of Clifton Avenue, but even there parcels large by modern standards were the rule, and even the 10-12 acre "building lots" in the Clifton of this period remained substantially larger than the equivalent building lots available in the city or its northern suburbs, between Cincinnati and Clifton. Clifton was in the country, and it was as the country that those first non-farming Cliftonites approached the land they began to acquire in the late 1830s.

The first of these appears to have been William G. T. Gano, who purchased some 60 acres of land in section 16, originally owned by Elijah Wood and then by Charles Fisher, in 1838. Gano was Cashier of the Lafayette Bank which held a mortgage in the amount of $40,800 on the old Mack lands in section 21, then owned by Charles Clarkson, and it was this connection which must have interested Gano in acquiring nearby real estate at $60 an acre, on the chance of selling it at something close to the value which the Bank placed on Clarkson's land, almost $400 an acre. It may have been Gano's own ownership of property in section 16 after 1838, which led him as an officer of the Bank, to approve an additional loan to Clarkson of $59,000 in the form of a mortgage on Clarkson's holdings north of McAlpin in sections 21 and 22, adjacent to the Gano holding.

Alternatively, Gano may simply have had the vision to recognize that this hilltop land in Clifton offered splendid opportunities for Cincinnati's newly rich to build summer homes in the country, villas on estates appropriate to their status as the social and intellectual and financial elite of what was indeed the Queen City of the West. Profit for the Bank and for himself must surely have seemed possible. Cincinnati's elite were moving out into the country, and hilltop land all over the county was rapidly increasing in value. But whatever the case may have been, it should come as no surprise that a number of the Bank's Directors, including George K. Schoenberger, Salmon P. Chase, and George Carlisle, and of their associates, including Buchanan and the Resors, soon began to invest in Clifton real estate, and some to build their homes on the ridge. Then, as now, those who like to work together like also to live together and to do business together. In the mid-19th century, they tended also to invest in real estate together.

Gano's own purchase was in any case the seminal act in the emergence of Clifton Village, and the transformation of Clifton from country to suburb, for between 1838 and 1844 he interested a number of his business associates and social peers in Clifton as a residential community. Some, like Robert Buchanan, first built summer houses, to escape from the heat of the city and to protect themselves and their families from the endemic and epidemic diseases, including Autumnal Fever and the dread Cholera, which threatened the health of Cincinnati's citizens during the warmer months of the year. Others, including Gano, appear to have begun the construction of permanent homes at the outset. Still others, like Flamen Ball, a prominent Democratic politician and later U. S. District Attorney for the Cincinnati District, appear to have acquired and remodeled older homes on their properties. Still others appear to have bought simply on speculation, especially those who acquired land in the northern half of section 21 after the Lafayette Bank foreclosed on Clarkson's mortgages in 1842, and after they had subdivided the land and run an access road connecting the Cumminsville Pike with the head of Clifton Avenue the following year. They called this new road after the subdivision they had created, which they named after themselves: Lafayette Avenue.

Among those who first purchased land in the Lafayette subdivision were many of Cincinnati's most prominent and powerful citizens, and its most active and astute investors: Salmon P. Chase, at the time an Associate Justice of the U. S. Supreme Court and later Chief Justice, who bought land across the street from his partner, Flamen Ball; Henry Probasco, who had married the boss' daughter and found himself in partnership with his brother-in-law, as a member of the firm of Tyler Davidson & Co., Importers and Jobbers of Hardware, Cutlery and Metals, one of the largest suppliers of tools and materials to Cincinnati's emerging metal-works industry, who bought a lot on the south side of Lafayette which he later found unsuitable for the construction of his grand mansion, "Oakwood"; Justice John McLean,

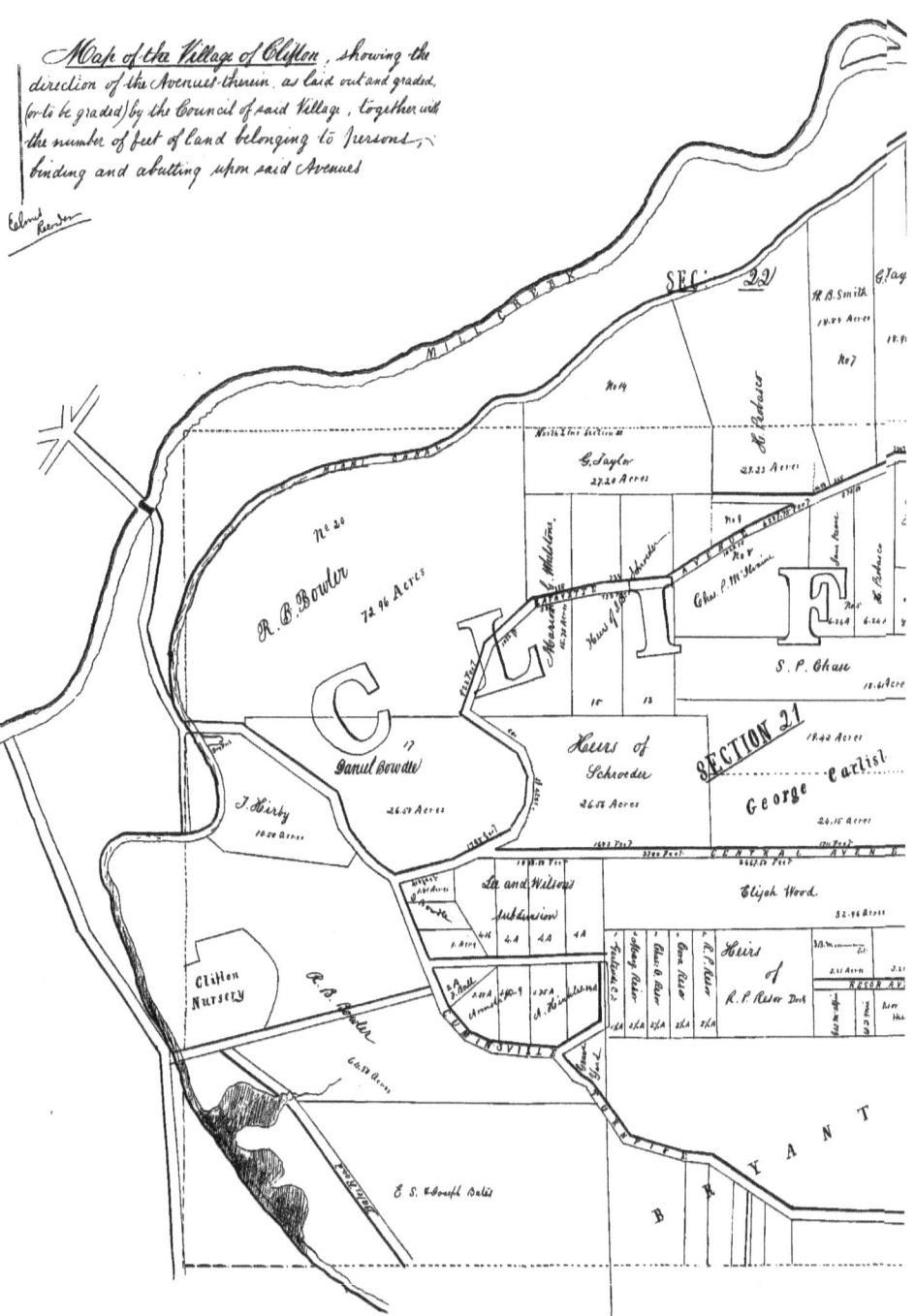

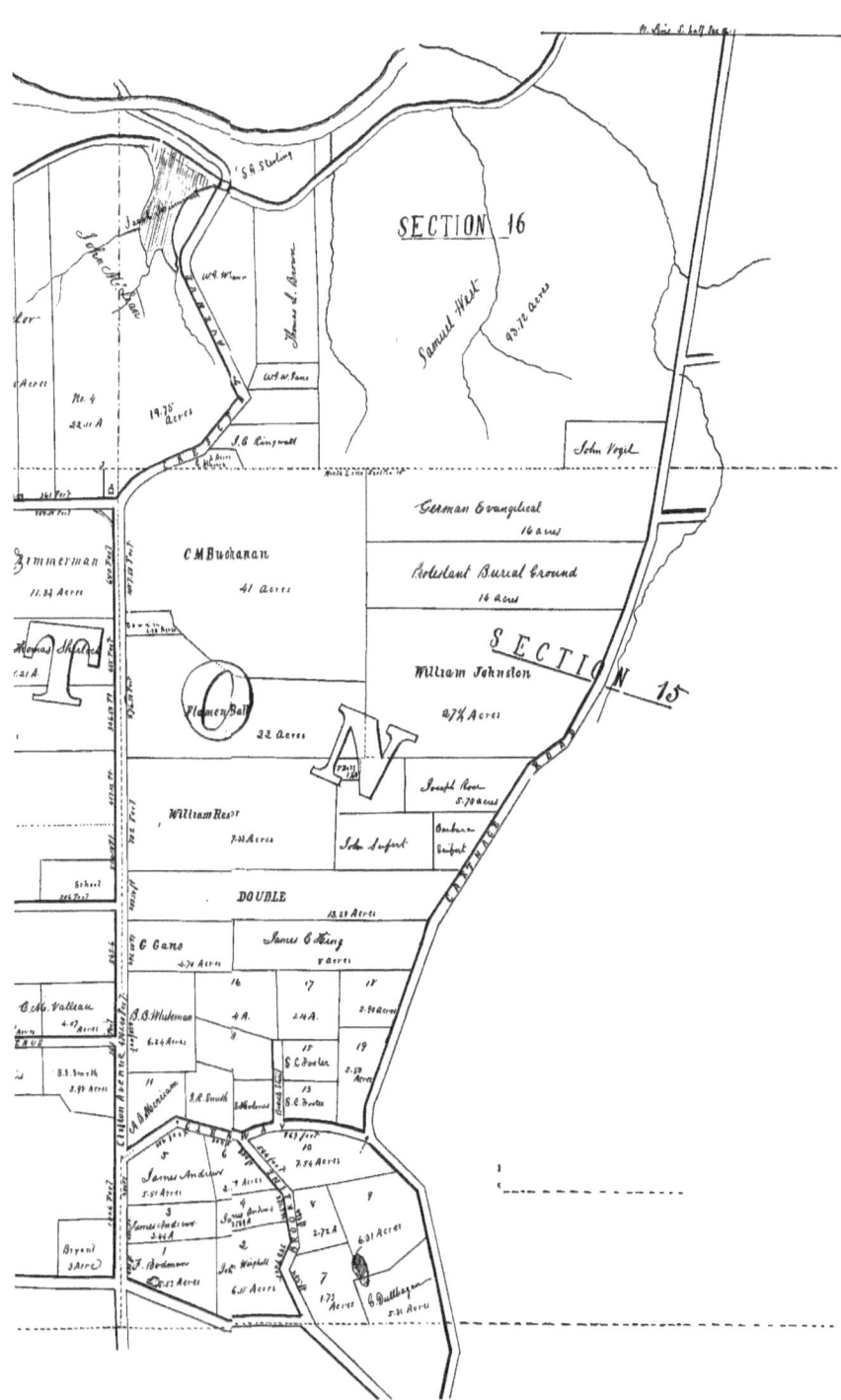

another Associate Justice of the U. S. Supreme Court, who acquired land in sections 22 and 16, on either side of the head of Clifton Avenue past the intersection of Lafayette; John Aston Warder, Editor of the *Western Horticultural Review,* and perhaps the moving force behind the landscape-gardening movement in Cincinnati, was himself an active geologist and paleontologist, interests which led him to participate in the affairs of the Western Academy of Natural Sciences (of which Buchanan was President) and to extensive speculation in Kentucky mineral lands; Episcopal Bishop Charles P. McIlvaine, who organized the "Clifton Chapel" at the head of Clifton Avenue, at which he conducted services until a permanent clergyman could be appointed, which later became the Calvary Episcopal Church; Griffin Taylor, President of the Cincinnati Equitable Insurance Co.; and Robert P. Bowler, proprietor of the Kentucky Central Railroad, whose property at the northwest corner of section 21, on which he constructed the grand home called "Mount Storm," afforded the best view of the railroad yards in the Valley, in which he had such substantial interest.

It was not until the mid-50s that these moved to Clifton, only after the Ganos and the Balls and the Buchanans and the Resors had demonstrated that Clifton's hilltop could be, and indeed had become, a pleasant place to live. Between 1843 and 1847, these families had all established themselves as Clifton's leading citizens, not in small part by constructing Clifton's largest houses or by remodeling their early cottages to meet the needs of year-round residence. And with their coming came others. Reuben P. Resor acquired some 40 acres from Elijah Wood, who may himself have built a permanent home at this time, on which Resor built first a summer home and then, a decade later, the grand Italianate home known at the beginning of this century alternatively as "Miss Ely's School" and, by the less respectful, as "Rat Manor." In 1843, B. B. Whiteman, President of the Merchant and Manufacturers' Insurance

> SALMON P. CHASE *forged a distinguished and lengthy political career, eventually serving in Lincoln's Civil War cabinet as Secretary of the Treasury. But he began his career in Cincinnati as an abolitionist lawyer, fueled in part by the 1836 Cincinnati Riot, in which anti-abolitionists destroyed the abolitionist press of James G. Birney.*

Company, acquired land the easy way, by purchasing 6.25 acres fronting on Clifton Avenue from Anne Marshall, in 1843 at about the time of his marriage to Mrs. Marshall's sister, Henrietta.

Whiteman's was the first of the "small" lots in Clifton. In 1851, Mrs. Marshall subdivided the "Hilltop Farm" property into twenty or twenty-one parcels, the largest of which, between Brookline and Ruther south of Glenmary, was some 7.5 acres, the smallest of which, on the east side of Biddle where it ran into Glenmary, was just under 2.5 acres. In 1853, first steps were taken in the subdivision of the Bryant property on either side of the Cumminsville Turnpike. The Resor property west of Clifton was subdivided following Reuben P. Resor's sudden death in 1854. Elijah Wood and Crafts J. Wright, who owned the property just north of the middle-line of section 21 later acquired by George Carlisle and J. B. Schroeder must have planned the subdivision of their respective parcels at this time also, for each donated a fifty foot strip of land running west from Clifton Avenue to Clifton Village for the construction of a new road, which could provide access to new home sites along its route.

Average cost of Construction in Cincinnati, 1875:

Lumber per M, $25
Brick per M, $6.50
Lime per barrel, $.90
carpenter / day, $2.50
mason / day, $3.50
painter / day, $2.50
laborer / day, $1.50
2 horse team / day, $4.00

$46.40

Columbus: *$46.25*
New York City: *$56.75*
Philadelphia: *$46.75*
San Francisco: *$51.00*

Called "Central Avenue" (now McAlpin), this new road ran along the line dividing section 21 in half, but it was "central" in more ways than this, for it provided the critical cross-street to Clifton Avenue, and hence helped define the Clifton community. During the 1850s, the intersection of Clifton and Central became indeed the center of the Village, figuratively as well as literally, for on this corner was located the Clifton School and the Clifton Village Hall, and it was only the insistence of the Cliftonites that their Village retain its residential character, that a central business district was prevented from growing up at this place.

The construction of Central Avenue may be said to have had importance of other kinds as well. In later years, it served as a dividing line between the northern half of Clifton, characterized by grand homes on large lots, and Clifton's southern half with its more modest, though still substantial houses on smaller lots, its first apartment buildings, and its business strip along Ludlow Avenue. Those are differences of the later 19th century however, but even immediately Central Avenue suggested the emergence of a new kind of Clifton, for it was the first publicly constructed road in the Village which didn't go anywhere, but was designed rather to provide access to the building lots on either side.

As new people sought to buy and build in Clifton, such access became increasingly important, and as access to the land was provided new people sought to buy and build in Clifton. And all the while the city of Cincinnati was pushing beyond its original boundaries, trying to catch up with its own population. New means of transportation, including the Cincinnati, Hamilton, and Dayton Railroad which served as a commuter railroad as well as a through line, and which connected with horse-cars and later the electric cars, made the suburbs possible after 1851 even as they tied the suburbs in more fully to the city, and thereby acted as the city's arms by which it reached out and pulled itself into the country.

The subdivisions of the early 1850s, including the sale of smaller parcels north of Central Avenue on both sides of Clifton, looked to making lots for homes available, and hence precipitated the definition of Clifton as a residential community. The grand country estates developed in the mid-40s remained, but in among them were constructed newer homes in different styles, their floor plan and their details, their location and their landscaped grounds designed to meet the needs of a suburban rather than a rural population. The houses themselves, like their owners, were of the city but not in it, yet it was with ultimate reference to the city that the new Clifton of the second half of the century emerged.

This transformation of the 1850s both followed from and required changes in the organization of Clifton but, as in all such transformations, what came first is not entirely clear. We may note, however, that from about 1850, Clifton both needed and could provide itself with public services of a variety of kinds—roads, sewers, fire and police protection, a school. Before 1850, such services could be provided by the residents themselves, whose number was small enough in any case to make self-help and voluntarism in mutual assistance both possible and appropriate. After 1850, as the population of Clifton grew the needs of that population also grew, and changed to needs which only a public corporation could provide. This happened, however, only after Clifton was incorporated as a public entity, and hence had the ability to meet those needs in the appropriate way; but, as we shall see, the very fact of Clifton's incorporation provided it with a new definition of itself as a location where such public services ought to be available.

With the growth of population after 1850, with the subdivisions of "farms" into "estates" and "estates" into building lots, with incorporation as a municipality, with the extension of public transportation facilities tying Clifton more closely to Cincinnati than to Cumminsville, Clifton thus emerged as "just another" suburb of the city. Although its leading citizens even in those days decried the changes which they had themselves helped to bring about, and looked back over so short a time as a decade with a sense of the golden past, it was only a matter of time before Clifton would become in law part of the larger metropolitan area of which it was already a part in fact. Then the struggle to maintain the "special character" of Clifton would begin in earnest, and on new terms. For as Clifton became increasingly a part of Cincinnati, it also became available to a new generation of wealth and social prominence whose baronial residences on Lafayette Avenue, begun in the 50s and completed in the 60s, would seek to overshadow the more classic, less ornate mansions of the Buchanans and the Ganos and the Resors, who had themselves come to Clifton as to the country. The men of this new generation viewed Clifton differently, as a place from which to rule the city, rather than as a retreat from its problems, a place unto itself.

Incorporation and its Consequences:
The Emergence of a Suburb

The first Constitution of Ohio, written in 1802, provided for the establishment of municipal, commercial, and charitable corporations through a single paragraph, which stipulated that "every association of persons, when regularly formed, within this state, and having given themselves a name may, on application to the legislature, be" entitled to receive letters of incorporation, to enable them to hold estates real and personal, for the support of schools, academies, colleges, universities, and for other purposes."

The incorporation of the Village of Clifton, like the incorporation of any other entity, thus required a special act of the General Assembly. In the absence of a uniform municipal code, moreover, it was inevitable that the charters granted municipal corporations would vary widely, according to the desires of those petitioning and according to their abilities to convince or persuade the legislators of the legitimacy of their needs and desires. Clifton's petitioners to the legislature were Flamen Ball, William Resor, and John A. D. Burroughs, who effected the incorporation of Clifton by an Act of March 23, 1850, which provided terms favorable to what Clifton's first generation of residents must have felt were Clifton's needs.

In addition to defining the boundaries of the village, the Clifton Charter stipulated powers to the municipal government identical with those provided in the Act of February 16, 1839, "For the Regulation of Incorporated Towns," with the additional power to "assess the cost of improvements" of streets "as nearly equally as possible, upon the property fronting upon such street," and to collect such assessments through suit against property owners if necessary; created a Clifton School District with three directors to be elected by the freeholders, which "school or schools, directors and districts shall enjoy all the privileges, and be subject to and have the benefit of all laws and parts of laws regulating, affecting or controlling the common schools in the city of Cincinnati;" and provided that the first election of mayor and other officers under the Charter should be held on the first Monday in April—the regular election day—1850. An amendment to the act of incorporation, passed on March 22, 1851, provided that taxes levied for and by the municipality were to be paid to the County Auditor, who would then disburse funds as appropriate, and established the Clifton Election Precinct for all local and national elections. From 1850 until its annexation by Cincinnati in 1896, Clifton was governed under the provisions of this charter and its amendment, with such slight modifications to it as the municipal laws passed periodically by the legislature after 1852 required.

To say thus that Clifton was "governed," however, is perhaps misleading. Then, as now, the work of local government consisted primarily in the regulation of public behavior and in the provision of public facilities, particularly streets and roads, and in the regularization of the duties of municipal officials. The records of the Clifton Village Council bear this out, as in the ordinances of April 1859, which provided that the Mayor was to serve as superintendent of the town police and overseer of village roads, with the power to order street repairs not in excess of $50, and that the town marshal was to be appointed by the mayor, to receive a salary of $30 per month, and was to serve also as pound master and to collect fines from or arrest persons violating the criminal laws of Ohio and the ordinances of Clifton.

Other ordinances of this period are more "interesting" to modern readers. On April 11, 1850, for example, the Council sought to prevent immoral practices by forbidding anyone fourteen years or older to riot, fish, hunt, shoot, trade, barter, or quarrel on Sundays within the corporate limits. On May 3, 1852, as required by the Act of 1839 for the regulation of incorporated municipalities, the Council made it unlawful for anyone to keep "any tavern, coffee house, restaurant, ale house, porter house, ale ship, porter shop, grocery, confectionery, public garden (beer garden), or any house or any other place as a place of habitual resort for the sale, barter or exchange of any vinous, spirituous or fermented liquors, or any intoxicating drink or drinks whatever in any quantity or quantities less than one gallon," unless licensed by the county authorities, and prohibited the slaughtering of animals within the village unless performed in a building provided with gutters to catch the blood. By this same ordinance, it was made unlawful for any person to permit any liquid harmful to the health or comfort of the citizens to run in open sewers from a "house, factory, shop, lot, mill, or distillery."

In 1854, an ordinance was passed to prevent and punish the fast or immoderate riding of horses through the streets of Clifton, or the driving or propelling of vehicles at a rate faster than six miles per hour, and another ordinance making it unlawful for cattle, horses, swine, sheep or other animals to run at large in the village, and providing for the construction of a village pound and for the appointment of a pound-master. In 1859, the council sought to prevent injury to the streets and avenues of the town by regulating the traffic of overloaded vehicles and to prevent the establishment of any new cemetery or grave yard within the village and to prohibit burials within its corporate limits.

Perhaps the best indication of the changes which occurred in the decade after incorporation appear in the following tables, prepared from the enumerations contained in the Village Minutes, and from the Federal Manuscript Census. Although incomplete, they suggest the rapid growth in population, the extraordinary increase in the value of real estate, and the growing sophistication of a community which possessed more pianos and more carriages in 1860 than in 1855. At the same time, these data point to the stability of Clifton's limited remaining agricultural ventures, and a curious disparity between the number of carriages and the number of horses—125 horses in 1860 to 147 carriages. One other fact bears mention: in 1853, the number of foreign-born, adults and youth under the age of 21, amounted to better than 40% of Clifton's population. By 1856, foreign-born persons accounted for almost half of Clifton's population, and this trend continued. Better than 56% of Clifton's 1870 population were foreign-born or of foreign parentage. In 1880, the proportion had increased to something over 59%.

With the growth of population and the subdivision of land, Clifton came to be characterized by that quintessentially urban phenomenon, the vacant lot, which replaced the meadow and the hillside in the consciousness of Cliftonites. Of 55 persons whose names appear on the 1861 map of Clifton listing property owners reproduced above, only 26 appear actually to have lived on the land they owned, and 8 of these owned additional building lots besides the one they occupied. Twenty-nine owned one or more lots in Clifton but resided in Cincinnati or in one of Cincinnati's other suburbs. Data drawn from the 1869 property map yields much the same results. Of 69 persons, 34 lived on the land they owned, and 15 of these persons owned additional building lots in Clifton. Thirty-five others owned one or more lots in Clifton, but resided elsewhere. Clifton during the 1860's must have looked very much like every other suburb of that period, and it must have felt very much like any other suburb of the period. For one thing, it was no longer in the country.

Population
1850-1880

	Youth 5-21 M F	Adults M F	Total	House Holds	Voters	Native Born	Foreign Parents	Foreign Born
1850	135		200?	40?				
1851	125							
1852	54	126	384		56			
1853	90	114	425	59	60	250		175
1854	52	144	470	72	85	253		217
1855	114	115	518	75	89			
1856	64	166	585	87	86	314		271
1857	89	151						
1858	82	341						
1859	95	404						
1860	82							
1870	99		1104	391	291	485	235	384
1880	182		1102	165?		390	318	276

Tied to Cincinnati by the Hamilton, Dayton and Cincinnati Railroad, by a network of improved roads, and by an emerging network of street railways, by the occupations and interests, political and financial of its residents, who were for the most part subject to the same laws as citizens of Cincinnati, and who came flocking from the city itself to the more desirable hilltops surrounding it as building lots became available, Clifton came to see itself as a beleaguered community, intent at once on establishing and maintaining their own identity and their own institutions. The ordinances of the Village Council reflect this new concern, as well as the new complexity of life in the new Clifton of the 1860's, presenting new problems, and requiring new solutions to old problems. Vandalism, vagrancy, disorderly conduct became a concern of the town fathers, as earlier stray animals and unruly schoolboys had

Property
1850-1860

	Acres	Real Property	Personal	Total Value
1850	1126.25	$156,480	$	$156,480
1851	1118.25	169,040	37,752	208,792
1852	1060.75	179,250	74,268	253,518
1853	1055.65	195,390	157,316	352,706
1854	1065.99	375,250	148,402	523,652
1855	1059	383,900	95,622	479,522
1856	1027	397,940	127,218	525,158
1857	1040	427,730	186,240	613,970
1858	1004	413,220	221,470	634,690
1859				
1860		462,800	226.665	689,465

dominated their attention. New streets had to be paid for, old streets had to be repaired, and the electorate had grown large enough and diverse enough so that genuine political conflict had replaced personal conflict as an aspect of village life.

In 1862, the Village Council sought to provide for the apprehension and speedy punishment of vagrants, loafers, lewd, and disorderly persons. Such were to be apprehended, brought before the mayor or other magistrate and sentenced to 30 days at hard labor in the Hamilton County Jail. Persons committing acts against property or persons, or even intending violence of this sort, including those apprehended with burglar tools in their possession, and those setting fire to buildings, were to be sentenced to 60 days at hard labor, and bread and water. By an ordinance of 1864, persons destroying fruit or ornamental trees, plants, or vandalizing any church, school house, dwelling house, fence gate, or sign were to be punished by 30 days in jail or $20 fine or both.

This last may have been a threat to Halloween pranksters, but it suggests a sense of outraged propriety and a fear of violated safety not present in the consciousness of Cliftonites during the previous decades. By 1870, indeed, Cliftonites had much to lose. Ornamental and fruit trees, elaborate plantings on the grand estates, churches, and a school building, which some found inadequate, but which was Clifton's school nonetheless.

Clifton School and a Sense of Place

The first school in Clifton is said to have been located on the quarter-acre lot northeast of the intersection of Clifton Avenue and Lafayette Circle, which William G. W. Gano sold to the Directors of School District No. 6 in 1844 for the sum of 15 dollars. On this site a log school house, ten feet by thirty feet, is said to have been built, but whether instruction actually took place in this building is not clear. Following incorporation and the establishment of the Clifton School District, this quarter acre appears to have been transferred to the Village or to the Directors of the new School District. In 1854, it was rented at a rate of $2.50 per month, perhaps by the Village to the School District, but perhaps not, for in that year the Clifton Council thought it appropriate that "the lot owned by the village should be improved and used as a school lot, as it is not probable a more eligible situation can be obtained." Yet public instruction of some sort must have been provided, perhaps in the basement of the "Clifton Chapel" on the northwest corner of the intersection of Clifton and Lafayette Avenues, where the Council itself held its meetings. It is hard to believe that the citizens of Clifton after incorporation would have violated the laws of Ohio and their own expressed desires, and failed to provide for the education of the town's young people, who numbered in excess of 125 between the ages of 5 and 21, by 1850. It is even harder to believe that the voters of Clifton would have permitted the levying of a local tax averaging two mills per dollar of assessed valuation for school purposes if the funds thus collected were not spent.

In 1854, in any case, the matter of schools came before Council, and attracted the particular attention of William Resor, who proposed that he would finance the construction of a new school building if an appropriate lot of 3-5 acres could be obtained by the Council. A committee was appointed to investigate the possibility, and reported back on March 4, 1854, that C. F. Wright had offered to sell a 3.25 acre parcel north of Central Avenue at its intersection with Clifton Avenue for $3,700, but that no subscribers to a school fund had been forthcoming. Whether Resor then went to the people or the people went to the Council is not certain, but at a public meeting on March 25th, the following resolutions were passed and transmitted to the Village Council:

Whereas a school of a high literary character in which shall be taught by the most approved methods, all the branches of a complete English education, including the Natural Sciences and Mathematics, is not only of great importance in regard to the instruction of youth, but imminently tends to advance the best interests of the community: It is therefore resolved. That such a school be established in the village of Clifton.

Resolved. That the thanks of the people are due to William Resor for his liberal offer to construct a schoolhouse, which shall not cost less than $2500 if the people of the village will purchase a suitable lot for the same containing not less than three acres.

Resolved. That we will accept the offer of Mr. Resor and pledge ourselves to raise by voluntary contributions a sufficient amount to purchase at least three acres of ground for a school lot.

Resolved. That the deed be taken for the lot by some person to be hereafter named, with such conditions and trusts as shall secure the great object of the donors, a school of the highest class and dignity; and which shall secure the confidence and respect of all intelligent persons.

Resolved, That as an evidence of the respect which the people bear for the liberal contribution of Mr. Resor the school shall be called "The Resor School of Clifton".

Resolved. That these proceedings be presented by the Chairman to the village council with the request of the people that they may receive their sanction, and be entered in the minutes.

In response to this resolution, a new committee of Council was appointed on April 1, 1854, to negotiate the terms under which Wright would sell one or more acres to the village for corporation purposes, and a resolution adopted authorizing the sale of the old school lot to Richard Bates. By June of that year, the transfer of the school lot to John Bates, Richard Bates' assignee, had taken place, and the acquisition of the Wright property for "corporation purposes" was in process. Soon thereafter, construction of a two-story brick building had begun, authorized by the trustees of the new Resor Academy and Clifton Literary Institute.

The Resor Academy property rapidly emerged as the center of Clifton civic life. In addition to the school and a public hall, outside the building was the Village Pound where the Marshall, who was installed in a house nearby, in his capacity as pound-master brought stray animals for safekeeping and, we may presume, for the delight of the school children. How their teacher, S. G. Sterling and his colleagues felt about the proximity of hogs and horses to this center of culture in Clifton we may also imagine.

By 1868, the existing building seemed inadequate to the developing needs of the community and the municipality. In that year a petition was presented to the Village Council requesting that the property be improved. "The undersigned freeholders and citizens of said Village of Clifton respectfully request that you pass an ordinance, levying a tax on the residents of said Village, sufficient to build an addition to the present Village School, as may enable the children of the residents of said village to attend, the present being inadequate to contain all who would wish to attend. The daily attendance as reported by Mr. Sterling the principal of said school is 71 and sometimes as many as 40 scholars are in one room. We also desire to increase the capacity of the Hall, so that it will be more suitable for public meetings."

In response to this request, the Board of School Directors was asked to report to the Council as to the necessity of purchasing a new lot and erecting a new school house, but no further steps were taken that year. Again in 1869, the residents of the village petitioned the Council to improve the school facilities:

> *To the Honorable City Council of the Village of Clifton: Your petitioners, resident freeholders within the corporate limits, most respectfully and earnestly solicit such action of the Council as will result in the immediate improvement of our School House and Public Hall. We fully appreciate the importance and necessity of furnishing to Clifton the very best educational advantages and the comforts and pleasure of a commodious Public Hall as well as an ambition not to be outdone in good works by neighboring corporations, encourages us to believe that your Honorable body will adopt a most liberal policy on this subject.*

This time the Council took more decisive action. The members of the Board of Trustees of the Resor Academy and Clifton Literary Institute and the Board of Education of the Village of Clifton (the School Directors) were invited to attend a special meeting of the Council to consider "the improvements of the Academy property, the wants of the village in regard to schools and the condition of the Public School of Clifton." Subsequent to this meeting, the Trustees of the Resor Academy and Clifton Literary Institute notified the Council of their intention to construct a new building, and offered to rent the Academy property to the Village. The Council accepted the offer, and a lease was signed dating from October 1, 1870. Mayor Hosea outlined the terms of the agreement and presented a description of the newly constructed building in his Annual Report for that year:

> *For many years past our citizens have felt the inadequacy of our school buildings, as well as our great want of a proper town hall, in which to hold lectures, public meetings, etc. Happily, this want has now been met. During the past fall, an arrangement was consummated with the incorporation of the "Resor Academy and Literary Institute of Clifton" by which they contracted to erect on their lot, which is centrally situated, a first class Academy building with ample accommodations for all the purposes of the Village at a cost of about $40,000, for which purpose they issued their bonds secured upon the property. The conditions were that the village should lease the premises for a term of fifteen years at an annual rent of $4000. The entire property, with the public pound lot and the cottage occupied by the Marshall to be included in the lease.*
>
> *The Village also agreed to purchase and hold $5000 of the bonds of the company, and as they are at 8% per annum, the rental of the property is thus reduced to $3600 per year.*
>
> *The Academy is an ornamental building in the Italian style, and is found to be well adapted to the uses for which it is intended. Besides four large rooms on the first floor for the schools, it has a fine Council Hall with a safe for the public records. The second floor which is reached by a large double stairway from the front, contains a public hall capable of seating 500 people, and three adjoining ante rooms. The whole building is warmed by furnaces,*

well ventilated, and lighted by gas made on the premises. A clock adorns the tower, which not only gives the correct time to all the village, but marks the passing hours upon dials in each school room and the public hall. In the basement is a strong "lock up" of which rogues will do well to take notice.

The completion of this enterprise so creditable to our citizens was signalized by proper ceremonies upon the dedication of the building followed by an inauguration ball which was attended by over 300 persons. Lectures and public entertainments have been arranged by the citizens for every Friday evening and your honorable body has by resolution authorized the Mayor to open the Hall on Sunday evenings to any of our citizens who may wish to use it for Divine Service, and it is now regularly used for that purpose.

Under the active management of our school Trustees, new vigor has been infused into that department, and with the able corps of teachers now employed, I see no reason to doubt that our school will rank with the best schools in the country. Whether it will be desirable to establish a graded school or add a higher department will be for the consideration of the school Trustees.

A new lease of the Academy property was executed by the Resor Academy and Literary Institute of Clifton to the village of Clifton in the fall of 1880. The village then subleased the rooms in the Academy building used for public school purposes to the Board of Education of the village of Clifton. This lease was for a term of 27 years, at an annual rent of $1800, and included light, heat, and the services of a janitor.

These agreements were still in effect when the village of Clifton was annexed to the city of Cincinnati in 1896, along with the villages of Linwood, Westwood, Riverside, and Avondale. As provided by state law, the school districts of these villages were incorporated into the Cincinnati school district and placed under the control of the Cincinnati Board of Education. The City of Cincinnati assumed the lease of the Academy property from the Resor Academy and Literary Institute of Clifton to the village of Clifton; the Board of Education of the Cincinnati School District assumed the lease of the school rooms of the Academy building from the village of Clifton to the Board of Education of Clifton Special School District. Clifton was placed in Ward 31 along with the newly annexed village of Avondale, and consequently the two villages shared representation on both City Council, and on the Board of Education.

While Clifton was developing its public facilities and protecting itself against vagrants and vandals, it also sought to develop a sense of

THE RESOR ACADEMY AND CLIFTON LITERARY INSTITUTE
Clifton and Central (McAlpin) Avenues, as it appeared in 1898. Built 1869-70, torn down in 1904-05

itself as a special kind of suburb. Its sense of community was institutionalized in the Resor Academy and Clifton Literary Institute, built by one citizen for his fellows, on land purchased by the people for their own use and the use of future generations. And the citizens themselves, as private individuals, were engaged in efforts at community betterment as they constructed their grand homes and planted them round about with trees and bushes, making a civilized park of what had been a ragged wilderness not a generation before. In 1868, Henry Probasco urged the Council to complete the process, by making provision for side-walks ("road walks") of limestone to make all parts of the village accessible to the pedestrian, for the sake of health and for the aesthetic pleasure which walking in Clifton would provide. With walks and additional plantings in public places, Probasco argued, Clifton could be as beautiful as Oxford or Cambridge.

The following year, in his farewell address to the people as he retired after almost twenty years of service as Mayor of Clifton, Flamen Ball himself completed Probasco's image. "Comprising as it does, some 1200 acres, and adorned as it is, with rare and beautiful trees and shrubbery, and with costly and elegant buildings," said Ball, Clifton could become "the largest and most beautiful park in the United States, if not in the world," a place of repose for its residents, and a delight to the citizens of Cincinnati, who could enjoy its pleasures without incurring the cost of the parks then being built by the city on its hill top lands.

Even as Ball spoke, however, and as he well knew, the annexation of Clifton by Cincinnati was being discussed. It was not the annexation of a park that the City Fathers of Cincinnati sought however, but additional population which could be counted into Cincinnati's total at the next Federal Census, and additional tax revenues from the valuable real estate on the hilltop. The annexation of Clifton, indeed, was but part of a larger plan of municipal improvement and territorial growth which had been presented to the City Council in November, 1868, and approved by that body in January of 1869.

Annexation and the Idea of Suburb

What Cincinnati's City Council proposed was special legislation designated as general legislation. It sought to obtain from the Ohio General Assembly modifications of the Ohio Municipal Code which would increase the powers of "all cities of the first class having a population of over one hundred and fifty thousand inhabitants" in certain specified areas. As the Cincinnati City Fathers well knew, only one city in the State—their own—met this description.

The additional powers they requested were to permit Cincinnati to issue bonds for the improving of avenues, for the construction of sewers, for the purchase and improvement of wharf property, and for the lease, purchase, or condemnation of property for park purposes; to deduct the increased value of property fronting on improved roads from the taxable value of such property; to have the tax assessors appointed by the county auditor instead of being elected by the citizens; and most important from Clifton's point of view, "to enlarge the corporate limits by acts of their Councils, so as to include incorporated villages."

No provision had been made in the Ohio Constitution of 1802 for the annexation of territory to or by any municipality. At the beginning of the nineteenth century, indeed, the very idea that any town or village might grow beyond its current, extensive boundaries, must have seemed outside the realm of possibility, and as late as 1839, the Act "for the regulation of incorporated towns" was silent on the subject of annexation.

The growth of population in Cincinnati, at least, and the northern extension of the city's residential area across Liberty Street to the bottom of the surrounding hills, and then up to the top of those hills, created the need for at least informal relationships between the "northern liberties" and the city itself before the mid-century. Annexation of this territory to the city seemed inappropriate. Establishment of the Northern Liberties as a separate municipal corporation, on the other hand, ran counter to the reality of continuity between the city and its first "suburb" and the easy flow of population across the Liberty Street boundary. A middle way was found in the establishment of the lower tier of sections in the Mill creek Township, between "the Lebanon Road" on the east and the Mill Creek on the west as the "Special Road District of Mill creek Township" in order to make possible the improvement of streets and roads in and out of Cincinnati itself.

By 1848, this arrangement seemed unsatisfactory, both to the residents of the Special Road District and to the residents of Cincinnati, who petitioned the Ohio Legislature to ascertain whether the residents of the Special Road District preferred the incorporation of their area as a town or annexation by and to the city of Cincinnati. The Act Relating to the Special Road District of Mill Creek Township, of February 18, which asked this question, also established rules for the process of annexation, which required majority votes of the qualified freehold voters in both the annexing territory and the territory to be annexed.

The citizens of the Special Road District voted for annexation in April of that year. In April, 1849, the citizens of Cincinnati voted for annexation also, and the end of that month the merger of territory was complete. Cincinnati now extended beyond Liberty Street to McMillan Street on the southern edge of the Clifton ridge. Whether this first expansion of Cincinnati beyond its original borders was the precipitating factor in the movement for the incorporation of Clifton as a town is unclear. From at least 1850, however, the citizens of Clifton kept a close eye on what the city was up to.

Yet they need not have worried, and indeed may not have worried, for the Ohio Legislature's "Act to Provide for the Organization of Cities and Incorporated Villages," passed on May 3rd, 1852, pursuant, to the requirement in Ohio's new Constitution of 1851 that the legislature regulate municipalities by "uniform laws," seemed to assure that annexation could not take place without the concurrence of the voters in the territory to be annexed, and provided only for the annexation of contiguous territory. Clifton was still safely separated from the city by a mile.

Under the 1852 law, annexation could take place in two ways: by petition of the citizens of the territory to be annexed, on concurrence of the municipal council of the annexing town or city; or at the instance of the council of the annexing town or city, provided that a majority of voters in the territories annexing and to be annexed each separately approved the proposed action. In either case, annexation was to be supervised by the county courts, which were to validate the petition or the election results, and had the power to annul annexations carried out improperly.

In the context of this 1852 legislation, and such annexations as had occurred under its terms (the annexation of the Village of

Fulton, along the Ohio between Cincinnati and Columbia Township on petition of the citizens of Fulton in 1854, for example), the proposal of the Cincinnati Council of 1868-69 seemed—and was—a direct threat to the independence of Clifton, as well as a departure from traditional practice. Cincinnati proposed that annexation could occur at the instance of its Council without reference to the wishes of citizens in the territories to be annexed, and that non-contiguous as well as contiguous territory might be annexed. That would include Camp Washington and Lick Run, in sections 31, 32, 25, and 26 of Mill Creek Township, which touched Cincinnati only corner to corner (and which was annexed under the 1869 annexation law, on November 12, 1869). It would also include Clifton, Walnut Hills, Columbia Township, Cumminsville (north of Camp Washington), Carthage, Green and Spencer Townships, and the "Northeast Precinct" of the Mill creek Township (Roselawn).

Clifton's response to this proposed annexation was straightforward. They questioned the motives of their sister municipality and its leaders. They insisted that they were content, and stood to lose rather than gain from inclusion in the emerging metropolis. And they insisted that annexation under the terms proposed by the Cincinnati Council was and would be illegal.

As early as January 23, 1869, a meeting was held to assess the sense of the people of Clifton on the subject of annexation, at which Henry Probasco offered the following preamble and resolutions which were unanimously adopted.

> *Whereas, The people of Clifton have learned through the newspapers that the Mayor of Cincinnati and the City Council thereof have without consultation with other corporations deeply interested therein, projected a proposed law to be presented to and adopted by the General Assembly of Ohio, to enable the City Council to extend the corporate limits of said city to an extent of more than one hundred square miles, so as to include the townships of Storrs, Delhi, Green, Mill creek, Spencer and the greater part of Columbia including the incorporated villages of Riverside, Westwood, College Hill, Clifton, Avondale, Camp Washington, Cumminsville, Carthage, Woodburn, and Columbia and*

Whereas, It seems to be the determination of the Mayor and Council of Cincinnati to procure the passage of said law it is now, by the people of Clifton, in town meeting assembled, convened to consider this project.

Resolved that we are opposed to said law upon the following grounds:

First- Because we do not desire to be forced into another municipal jurisdiction without our consent.

Secondly- That we are subject to law of Incorporation dated as far back as 23 March 1850 whereunder we have conducted our municipal government with which government we are still satisfied.

Thirdly- We believe the General Assembly has no more power to authorize the city of Cincinnati by its own will to annex Clifton and other municipal corporations to that city than they have to authorize Clifton to annex Cincinnati to its corporation.

Fourthly- That the enumeration of population to be made at the next national census in 1870, while it will nominally increase the population of Cincinnati should the surrounding country be annexed, will add nothing to the real wealth, business, influence or political power of the city or county either in Congress or in the State Legislature.

Fifthly- The plea asserted that most of the people of Clifton transact business in Cincinnati and thereby derive great benefits from their business in the city although true in substance, is nevertheless unsound in respect of the question of annexation because those people, on their real estate stores and manufactories, pay more taxes by many thousand dollars per year, on the duplicate of Cincinnati than they do on the duplicate of Clifton.

Sixthly- The assertion that the people of Clifton need the protection of the city government of Cincinnati is absolutely untrue 1, Because that government does not now protect its own citizens within its present corporate limits from nightly highway robberies and other outrages. 2. Because it does not furnish a police, or the facilities of gas or water or a fire department as far north as the top of Vine Street Hill and we would be left without either while we are now protected by our own police and by our own arrangements for gas and water.

Seventhly- Because the city of Cincinnati is engulphed in a public debt of about four million dollars contracted for purposes not our own, and for which neither we nor any representative of ours ever contracted; and that in case our village should be forced into the city we would be obliged to pay our proportion of that debt with interest, without having derived any benefit therefrom.

Eightly- Because our village would cease to control our roads and avenues which have been built at our own expense, and are free to everyone, and are the best in the State of Ohio, and we would be obliged to submit to the dictation of a "City Council" who would by reason of the distance of those roads from the thickly settled parts of the city, suffer them to go to ruin.

Ninthly- Because we believe that such a sweeping law of annexation, conferring upon the City Council of Cincinnati the power to annex to that city neighboring corporations as high in dignity as itself, without the consent of such annexed corporations and without a vote of the people interested, would be in defiance with all the existing, laws on such a subject.

Tenthly- We believe that the power proposed to be conferred upon the City Council of Cincinnati would be dangerous to the morale of the people and that

HENRY PROBASCO, Clifton's fourth mayor, made his fortune in the hardware business partnered with Tyler Davidson, in whose name he dedicated the famous downtown fountain. He also gave to the citizens of Clifton the Probasco Fountain in 1888.

it might furnish to said Council the means of exercising a corrupt arbitrary and despotic authority over the city so proposed to be enlarged.

We have always desired the prosperity of Cincinnati and have done and expect hereafter to do all we can to perpetuate it, but we are unwilling to be overridden by our powerful neighbor or to be subjected to the control of its Council.

Temporarily, at least, these efforts were successful, for the Legislation passed by the General Assembly in May, 1869, required that a majority of voters in municipalities to be annexed concur in such annexation. Early in 1870, however, an amendment to the act of May, 1869, was introduced into the General Assembly and promptly passed. "An Act to Prescribe the Corporate Limits of the City of Cincinnati," dated April 16th, provided that annexation of any municipality was to depend on a majority vote of all the electors in the entire territory to be annexed. With the issue thus joined, the Clifton Village Council beginning in March, 1870, petitioned the Ohio Legislature to amend the bill before it, appointed a committee of three (Probasco, Sherlock, and Burgher) to "confer and cooperate with the committee appointed by the Avondale Council and other such committees as may be appointed by neighboring corporations on matters pertaining to the proposed annexation," and prepared information concerning the value of taxable real estate to be used by Clifton's attorneys in the struggle.

Lobbying and petition were of no avail, however. At a special election on May 16, 1870, the total vote of the citizens in the Mill Creek Township areas to be annexed was 1,125 for annexation, 1,082 against, although this included the votes of citizens of Spencer, Camp Washington, and Lick Run—communities which had been annexed under the 1869 law as passed by the Legislature. Clifton voted 103 to 30 against annexation, Avondale voted 130 to 97 against, Cumminsville voted 380 to 341 against, Columbia Township voted 78 to 46 against, and so on. At this point, Clifton, Avondale, and other communities joined in a suit to enjoin the completion of annexation, which was decided at the December, 1870, term of the Supreme Court of Ohio in favor of the villages. Messrs. Sage and Hinkle represented Clifton, Avondale and Cumminsville, and in April, 1871, received the thanks of the Village Council and a check for their services.

Cincinnati's attack on the independence of Clifton transformed Clifton's conception of itself. No longer a village separate from the city, increasingly surrounded by the city, a distinct municipality only through the carelessness of the authors of the 1870 Annexation Law, which was found unconstitutional as "special" rather than "general" legislation, Clifton came now to see itself as defined by the city itself, as a suburb. This new note appears first, perhaps, in Mayor Hosea's address to the Council and the Citizens of Clifton in December, 1870, when the issue of annexation's effect was not yet settled. But it was a theme which would persist. Clifton existed now only in relation to the larger metropolis of which it was, for better or worse, a part.

> *Our village is peculiarly situated. Covering about 1200 acres: its corporate limits adjoin those of Cincinnati upon the south from whose business center it is scarce three miles distant, yet no great public highway or turnpike road passes through it. Hence it is exempt from the inconvenience of the dirt, the mud, the droves of cattle, the long caravans of passing teams, and all other annoyances incident to a public thoroughfare leading into a great city. The topography of the country places it outside, or rather between the great lines of travel. The bold hills which hem it in on the north and project far out into the valley of the Mahketewah seem to invite the palatial residences which crown their summits, from whence are to be seen landscape views not excelled, if equalled, elsewhere in the world. Within the village proper, the gentle slope, the softly undulating lawn, the tasty cottage and the imposing villa, with every variety of shrub, plant, flower and evergreen, distinguish it as one of the most delightful suburban spots in the country.*

The New Clifton and Its Stately Homes

In many ways, 1870 marks the high point of Clifton's 19th century history. It had resisted annexation. It had been acknowledged in the Federal Census as a distinct social unit defined by a distinct geographic location. It had passed the peak period of growth during the 1860s, when its population had increased from under 700 to over 1100. After 1870, Clifton's population would level off, the value of its real estate would remain fairly constant, the rate of subdivision and construction of new houses would decline. At the same time, new concerns would absorb the attention of the Village Council—street repairs and maintenance, contracts for sewerage and later gas and electric service, street railway franchises, and especially politics—municipal politics, and school politics, and, as later would happen, these became intertwined.

One result of local politics was the emergence of Henry Probasco as Clifton's fourth Mayor, succeeding William H. Harbaugh, Flamen Ball, and Robert Hosea, and the new dominance of Clifton's "barons" both in the social and political life of the village, and in the consciousness of residents both of Clifton and of Cincinnati. For after this date it was the mansions on Mount Storm, rather than the older homes of the 1840s which came to symbolize Clifton and its relationship to metropolitan Cincinnati,

These changes in Clifton may most easily be seen, perhaps, by the difference between the style of mansions constructed in the earlier and later periods. While examples of both styles are imposing to modern eyes, and must have been intended to awe even in the 1850s, it is only the homes begun in the late 50s and completed in the 60s which truly strive for the monumental. If the houses of neither group may be said to be "modest," that is, the former at least suggest a kind of essential "modesty" about their builder-owners.

Fine examples of homes built in both periods still stand in Clifton. The William Resor house on Greendale Avenue, for example, was built about 1848 on 12 of Resor's original acreage, in the center of a plat running north 702 feet on Clifton Avenue from Woolper, and east from Clifton to the Carthage Road. The house is said to have been designed originally in the Greek Revival style using post and lintel construction, and subsequently remodeled in the 1860s through the addition of a third story and Mansard, and the extension of the dining room and parlor across the veranda which was enclosed on either side of the house. At this time, "modern" woodwork and mantels were added, an oak buffet and server were built into the dining room, and bookcases were built into the library. In 1893, when the "Greendale" estate—or what remained of it—was subdivided and Greendale Avenue cut running east from Clifton Avenue, the house is said to have been "moved" and "turned"—perhaps merely reoriented—to face the new street, perhaps by the addition at this time of the glassed gazebo and entrance porch now at the southeast corner of the house. East of the property were gardens and orchards, the outlines of which may still sometimes be seen by one who wanders through the back yards fronting on Greendale Avenue.

The Reuben P. Resor house, now at the north end of Cornell Place, was built in 1852-54 by William's brother in that extension of the Greek Revival style, the Italianate, and was the second Resor home constructed on this property west of Clifton Avenue on either side

WILLIAM RESOR HOUSE, *"Greendale," 254 Greendale Avenue, built ca. 1848. Remodeled ca. 1868, gazebo added ca. 1893*

REUBEN P. RESOR
HOUSE
*3517 Cornell Place
as it appeared in
1921.
Built 1853-54*

of Resor Avenue. An earlier house, located where St. John's Unitarian Church now stands, was built in the 1840s. During the 1850s, Reuben's brother Jacob is said to have lived there, and in the 1860s, the house and lot passed to Robert Hosea. Extensively remodeled as each new resident took possession, before it was torn down it bore little relationship to the country cottage which must have been its first form.

During the 1850s in any case, Reuben Resor determined to build the grandest home in what was then Clifton. With broad piazzas commanding a view of the Mill Creek Valley to the west and a largely open prospect to the east, the house was reached by a long drive, later Resor Avenue, which passed through stone columns (one of which may still be seen at the corner of Hedgerow Lane) to a flight of broad steps, at the top of which stood the house with its octagonal tower. About 1865, the house and 21.25 acres of the original Resor property were sold to David Gibson, a commission merchant and dealer in whiskey, flour and grain whose brother William, of the McCormick and Gibson Cincinnati Lead Pipe and Sheet Lead Company, built a home of his own on 16.33 acres south of Warren Avenue at about the same time. During the 1880s, the Resor house was sold to Seth Evans, one of the founders of the Second National Bank, who appears to have subdivided the western 12.25 acres into the Evanswood estates (named for himself and Elijah Wood, or perhaps for Evans' "woods") after running Evanswood Avenue as an access road. In later years, the house became the property of George Bartholemew and then the site of the Clifton School for Young Ladies, directed by Miss E. Antoinette Ely, and popularly known as "Miss Ely's School."

William Resor built "Greendale" about 1848. At about the same time, his friend and sometime associate Robert Buchanan, abandoned the summer cottage he had constructed in 1843-44, and began construction of "Greenhills" now on Lafayette Circle. Constructed in the Italianate style, it was originally L-shaped, although the addition of a library and porch on the northeast corner brought it to the more conventional rectangular dimensions, and details more characteristic of the 1860s than the 40s, were added. The original entrance was on the west side of the house and opened onto the drive which circled down to Clifton Avenue along the route of Lafayette Circle. From the side entrance (now the front door) on the south, a path may well have led as a short cut to the Greendale estate of William Resor, along the line of what is now Greenhills Avenue, which, if projected north would skirt the ridge which James Espy once owned, running east from Clifton Avenue just north of Calvary Episcopal Church, up the hill to Flamen Ball's property on either side of Rural Lane, and thence across to Greenhills itself. (It is nice to think of these two visiting, walking through their orchards together, discussing the affairs of the Village and of the City far to the south. Perhaps young Charles Buchanan joined them on their rambles, from his home on Clifton Avenue or Flamen Ball, who lived in the "old home" on Clifton Avenue, once occupied by Aaron Ireland, the original owner of the land, who had bought 32 acres in section 15 from Nicholas Longworth in 1826 for $275 and lost it in a sheriff's sale in 1843, when John Avery bought it for $1900 and sold it to Ball and Buchanan, who subdivided' and sold portions to James Espy and to the Calvary Episcopal Church, which bought its acre of land for $3000 in 1863.)

Compared to the white painted country homes built during this earlier period, with their orchards and vineyards reinforcing the bucolic air which had attracted that first generation of residents to Clifton in the mid-1840s, the homes built on Lafayette Avenue in the 60s were pretentious and consciously baronial, and were constructed with

Robert Buchanan house, *3874 Clifton Avenue, built ca. 1843*

Robert Buchanan house, *"Greenhills," 230 Lafayette Circle, built ca. 1848. Remodeled ca., 1868*

ultimate reference to the city from which they would be seen. Even today, surrounded by full-grown trees planted first in the 60s and 70s of the last century, when the landscape work around them was begun, their jutting towers punctuate the Clifton ridge, and make all know that here lived the lords of the land. The houses of the 40s were designed to be in the country. The houses of the 60s were designed to awe the city.

Foremost among these is "Oakwood", Henry Probasco's home designed in Romanesque-Gothic by architect William Tinsley, and constructed between 1859 and 1866 at a cost estimated to have exceeded half a million dollars. With formal gardens rather than orchards, with a rosarium containing four-thousand roses instead of vegetable beds, with exotic trees and shrubs brought from the Pyrenees, the Himalayas, and the Rocky Mountains instead of meadows, it was "Oakwood" especially which brought Clifton its designation as the "aristocratic suburb" par excellence. Its entrance hall, 15 by 70 feet, was decorated by frescoes painted by Francis Pedretti, who was brought to Cincinnati to work on the Probasco mansion and remained to decorate the homes of Probasco's peers. The grand staircase which leads into the tower is solid oak and took sculptor Ben Pittman three years to complete. "Oakwood" is simply the most imposing of the Mount Storm "castles," perhaps because it stands on the crest of the ridge and is now surrounded by more modest and more modern homes, in stark stone contrast to their warmer brick and stucco.

Henry Probasco House *"Oakwood"* *430 West Cliff Lane, built ca. 1859-67*

GEORGE K.
SCHOENBERGER
HOUSE
"Scarlet Oaks"
440 Lafayette
Avenue
Built ca. 1863-67

The George Schoenberger home, "Scarlet Oaks" west of "Oakwood" and nestled in the hillside, is no less impressive and cost considerably more to complete. Built on land acquired in the early 60s from George Taylor and the estate of J. B. Schroeder, "Scarlet Oaks" was said to have cost in excess of $750,000 by 1867 when the building itself was completed, exclusive of decoration and interior furnishings. A turreted, gargoyled, true-gothic showplace, it was designed by James K. Wilson.

"The Windings," constructed by William C. Neff on 25 wooded acres and designed as an exact replica of Kenilworth by the architect Thomas Sargent, was said to have been so expensive to maintain that Neff could not afford to live in it after the 70s. Completed in 1867, it was subsequently acquired by the Sisters of the Sacred Heart who used it as a convent and then as a school for young ladies.

The Neave house, built on the only "cleared" land along Lafayette Avenue when the Clarkson subdivision was made in 1842, and hence the most expensive of those hilltop acres unsuited for agriculture, stood on what appears to be the highest point in Clifton. Although a house was not built until the 1860s, the elevation of the land may well have caused Henry Probasoo to abandon his original plan for the construction of "Oakwood" on the south side of Lafayette, where it would be over-topped by his neighbor's home, and to acquire land across the street. Even then, however, he is said to have had extensive grading of the land carried out, so that "Oakwood" would stand on a knoll and thus compete with his uphill neighbors' dwellings. The Neave house, later acquired by H. R. Hunefeld, was built in the Romanesque style popularized by H. H. Richardson, and boasted one of the earliest swimming pools in Clifton.

The fascination with the Gothic in its many forms led Probasco, Schoenberger, and the others to choose William Tinsley, the architect of "Oakwood," to design a church appropriate to the community they were creating. Between 1866 and 67, Tinsley designed and supervised the construction of the Calvary Church on Clifton Avenue, in a compatible style to the mansions then just complete or under construction. Henry Probasco donated the 120 foot high stone tower and its bells as a memorial to his brother-in-law and longtime business associate, Tyler Davidson, and subsequently persuaded the building committee, of which he was chairman, to permit his own artist in residence, Francis Pedretti, to fresco the interior of the sanctuary. The Church was opened on January 19, 1868.

Is this all of Clifton architecture? Is it the best? Is it even representative? It is certainly not all, and whether it is the best is a matter of taste, and a sense of historical appropriateness. Even the Italianate villas of the 1860s, however—Robert Bowler's "Mount Storm" at the west end of Lafayette Avenue, and the handsome home of J. W. Ellis, the President of the First National Bank, at the end of what is now Middleton Court, aspired to a grandness not characteristic, of the homes built earlier. The monumental buildings of the 60s along 'Lafayette Avenue thus set a tone for the construction of the later "grand homes" of Clifton which, if they are not quite stately, nonetheless aspire to such monumentalism as was possible in a later era.

Perhaps the best example of these later houses is one not quite in Clifton, but at its southern edge: "Parkview," the home of Cincinnati's one-time political "boss," George B. Cox, who moved to join his political allies on the hilltop about 1895, at the time of Clifton's annexation to Cincinnati. "Parkview" was built on what may have been the site of the old Clifton House tavern, a not-quite respectable place much patronized by the respectable, as was "Parkview" itself, for Cincinnati's political elite came of necessity to do business with Cox at his new home, even while Clifton's social elite looked askance at the presence in their midst of such a newcomer to power and prominence as Cox appeared. Their own vision of historic Clifton, which provided them with a sense of their own social prominence, characteristically ignored the political past of most of Clifton's leading citizens.

After Cox's death in 1916, his wife Caroline is said to have become more and more reclusive, shunning the neighbors who shunned her first. Upon her death in 1938, it was discovered that she had willed "Parkview" to the Cincinnati Union Bethel as a home for girls.

GEORGE B. COX HOUSE
"Parkview"
Brookline and Jefferson Avenues
built 1895

The Short Road to Neighborhood

Clifton, said Robert Maxwell in 1870, "is purely a suburban place. There is nothing of the town about it. There is neither store, grocery, mechanic's shop, nor saloon, and the whole place is so completely under the control of those who desire to keep it for purposes of country residence, that it must be many years before the general character of the place can change. Of course, it will become more thickly settled. Each year the inhabitants will increase in numbers, until it will become less retired; but it will be among the last places about Cincinnati that will suffer from encroachments of business."

Even while the barons of Mount Storm were busy at the business of separating themselves from the city of which they were a part and which had created them, after 1870 the rest of Clifton proceeded to become more like Cincinnati and its other suburbs, even if its residents did take their sense of self from the doings along Lafayette Avenue. During the 1880s and 1890s, the Ludlow Avenue business strip emerged to serve what was now less a separate place than a "neighborhood" within the larger city. The remaining large lots in the southern half of sections 21 and 15 were now subdivided, and new streets were cut, graded, and Macadamized at the expense of the Village, to provide access to the new houses which would eventually be constructed. Now fewer and fewer of Clifton's residents followed the old, genteel pursuits of bankers and merchants. More were engaged in manufacturing, and even more were salaried employees, some blue collar, some white collar. Some worked as gardeners or domestic servants in the grand homes along Lafayette or on the older estates along upper Clifton Avenue. Most did not, but must have taken the streetcars to work outside of Clifton, then as now.

By 1896, in most respects, Clifton was the modern neighborhood, the modern city in microcosm. Eight men served in the fire department. Twelve men served in the police department, as "marshalls." A system of fire alarm boxes summoned help from the firemen, who operated a one-horse hose wagon, a one-horse hose reel, a hand hose reel, and 2100 feet of hose, though not all at the same time, and must have called out the police also, since the nine miles of insulated wire connecting the alarm system terminated in a box located at police headquarters. A varying number of men worked on the roads, using the village's two road plows, its two street-rollers, its three four-horse wagons, its three two-horse cars, its two one-horse carts, as well as appropriate quantities of stone, asphalt, and numerous hand tools owned by the Village. Taxes for improving the ten miles of village streets were sometimes paid and sometimes not paid. Contracts for supply of water and gas were sometimes negotiated to the satisfaction of the Villagers and sometimes not. Bonds were sometimes issued. Elections were sometimes disputed. Politicians sometimes called each other names, and sometimes were called names. Clifton had become modern.

Thus it was that, when in 1893 the City of Cincinnati once again attacked Clifton's independence through an attempt at annexation, Clifton's struggles were at once half-hearted and doomed to failure, for despite the legitimate protestations of her mayor and prominent citizens, that the so-called Lillard Law violated the Constitution of Ohio as had the legislation of April, 1870, the courts were unable to find convincing Clifton's arguments in defense of her continued independence from the city of which she was so much a part. Only later, when the particular issue of the annexation of Clifton and Avondale and the other suburbs had long been settled, did it seem important to anyone that a "legal" annexation law should be written, just to keep things on the up and up.

The Lillard Law was no more high-handed in its intent than the proposed act of 1869, which would have given Cincinnati the power to annex incorporated municipalities at its own instance. For reasons now not clear, the proposed legislation of 1893 passed the Ohio General Assembly, however, and that made the difference. By this new law, a vote on the annexation of an incorporated municipality was to require a majority of the combined votes cast in the annexing municipality and in the municipality to be annexed. Clifton was simply outvoted, and though she took to the courts once again, in the end her time had come. Between 1895 and 1896, annexation commissioners appointed by the county court examined the resources of Clifton, counted the horses and mules and wagons and school-desks belonging to the Village, evaluated the financial situation of the Village, and negotiated the terms of annexation, by which Cincinnati would assume the debts of the Village and accept responsibility for the fulfillment of existing contracts, including those written between the Village and her employees, and by which Clifton would become "Clifton," a neighborhood rather than the separate place she had ceased to be a decade or more before.

Clifton as Neighborhood: The Post Annexation Years

In May of 1975 the Clifton Town Meeting published *The Clifton Community Plan: Goals and Objectives*, which it described as the first report in a planning series. It was, in many respects, a conservative document, distinguished by repeated assertions of Clifton's uniqueness and of a determination to preserve the area's "village" character. The goals and objectives spelled out in the plan, however, looked to making the neighborhood neither unique nor village like. The plan comes down in favor of a heterogeneous residential community unfettered by restrictions against particular socio-economic, religious, racial or age groups; argued for the improvement of the Clifton-Ludlow business commercial district; urged the development of additional social service institutions for the local population and the retention of existing city-wide institutions which provided jobs for Cliftonites; suggested provision of both diverse educational opportunities within Clifton for individuals "throughout the life span" and a broad range of recreational facilities for individual and group activities; and looked toward a transportation network that would take through traffic around the village without disrupting or clogging its local travel patterns. With the exception of certain noxious land uses, such as drive-in or fast food restaurants and industries, which presumably would remain in

THE BELLEVUE HOUSE *welcomed commuters and tourists using the Bellevue Incline which connected riders to the outskirts of Clifton.*

somebody else's neighborhood, Clifton felt impelled to make itself virtually a city within a city in order to reach its "over-riding Goal; To Strengthen and Maintain the Residential Quality Unique to Clifton."

One might argue that this mood was not new, but dated to the period immediately after annexation and represented the stance which Clifton took after its strenuous efforts to stay out of the city had failed. That explanation rests on the assumption, however, that absorption into the city confirmed Cliftonites' most terrifying fears. Annexation meant, in this view, the acquisition of the most unsavory aspects of urban life through a diversification of the community which threatened to turn the suburb into a blighted area at best and a slum at worst. That kind of spectre might have provoked a defensive reaction on the part of Clifton planners who felt that only by having and controlling everything they needed for their conception of the good life could they save the place from being torn from its roots and changed irrevocably. None of those things, as it turned out, happened in the years immediately following annexation. Indeed, an older process by which Clifton was already turning from suburban into neighborhood status merely continued.

In this perspective the critical events in the transformation of Clifton came not in 1896, but between 1870 and 1880. Early in that decade two "incline planes" went into operation, one the Main Street or Mt. Auburn and the other the Bellevue or Clifton, each of them capable of hauling horse drawn street railways and other vehicles up the sharp faces of the hills around the basin. By 1880 horse-car lines running

Between 1872 and 1948, five inclines connected downtown Cincinnati to its hilltop neighborhoods. Bellevue Incline closed in 1926, and the last incline, Mt. Auburn, closed in 1948.

51

from the top of the inclines linked the once-remote hilltop suburbs directly with the street railway system which served the commercial, industrial, and residential complex in the basin. One line started at the Mt. Auburn incline terminal and proceeded by way of Auburn Avenue to Vine and Jefferson as far as Brookline on the eastern edge of Clifton. The other started at the Clifton incline and ran up Ohio and Calhoun to Vine, thence to Jefferson where it dead-ended at Brookline. Those transit improvements sparked the rapid settlement of Clifton Heights and Corryville, but Clifton proper still stood just beyond the system.

What remained of Clifton's isolation, however, ended in 1888. In that year the Cincinnati Street Railway Company, after receiving authorization from Clifton Village authorities, tied into the hilltop connections by running a cable line from Vine to Jefferson to Ludlow, north on Middleton to Bryant, east from Bryant to Telford, south on Telford to Ludlow, and back via Jefferson to Vine. The cable line then followed Vine down the hill through the Over-the-Rhine district, and into the central business district where it terminated at Fifth Street. In 1890, it took riders 25 minutes, including a transfer at the Jefferson-Vine powerhouse, to make the trip from Clifton to Fountain Square in the very heart of the city.

Within the next decade, both Clifton's early 20th century transportation network and the familiar outlines of its contemporary land use pattern had already taken shape. In 1896, the moment of annexation, streetcar lines stretched along Ludlow down to the Miami and Erie Canal and along Vine as far out as Mitchell. As in 1888, one branch of the system also penetrated the southern edge of the neighborhood, only now it not only formed a loop around the Ludlow, Middleton, Bryant and Telford block, but also ran up Middleton to McAlpin and over to a dead-end on Clifton. All the non-residential addresses in Clifton, except for a florist on McAlpin (Gustav Adrian, prop.), lay close to the street car lines which etched the periphery of the neighborhood. At the bottom of Ludlow hill, near the canal, sat a boat building establishment, a combination saloon and grocery, and a florist. Farther east on Ludlow, beyond McAlpin and Evanswood, came the Jewish cemetery. From there nothing broke the residential continuity until one reached the corner of Ludlow and Clifton. There a saloon stood on the south side of Ludlow half a block west of Clifton, and across the street stood a confectioner and two groceries. A drug store on the northeast corner of Clifton and Ludlow and a candy manufacturer on the south side of Ludlow closer to Clifton Avenue than Brookline completed the neighborhood shopping district. Not far from there, on the corners of Clifton and Senator Place and Clifton and Bryant, stood respectively the Methodist and Presbyterian churches. The only other businesses lined the east side of Vine Street, starting with two florist shops, a marble works, and a saloon concentrated, and perhaps not fortuitously, in the vicinity of the German Evangelical Protestant Cemetery. Farther north, on Mitchell near the canal, stood a brick manufacturer and another saloon, and on Harriet between Kesslar and Vine, a shoemaker. This arrangement left the entire center of the neighborhood residential.

A decade and a half later, after the population had edged up from 3,555 to 5,540, the incidence of non-residential land use had become more frequent, but the pattern remained precisely the same. The lower end of Ludlow near the canal now contained six business addresses, all of them below the intersection of Lafayette and Ludlow, and only the Jewish cemetery, a business at Lyleburn, and a professional office on Whitfield just off Ludlow, interrupted the residential character of the street as far up as Middleton. By this time, however, the business-commercial strip from Middleton to Brookline had filled out considerably. That strand accommodated 19 businesses on both sides of the street, including Fenton dry cleaners and Stier's drug store. Sprinkled among them stood, for the first time, apartment buildings, five of them along the Ludlow commercial strip. Three others were located on Middleton, one at the corner of Shiloh, another at Bryant, and the last at Resor. Another stood on Hosea at Clifton Avenue and the last on the south side of Hosea one-third of the way to Brookline. The streetcar routes followed the same paths as in 1896, and all the commercial places and apartments on or near the strip huddled close to the mass rapid transit facilities. Most of the rest of the businesses lay along Vine, three clustered at the southern extreme near Ludlow, sixteen on either side of Woolper south of the German Evangelical Cemetery, and five between Glenwood and Wuest on northern Vine Street in St. Bernard. Except for the florists on McAlpin and Biddle, a professional office on McAlpin, a business on Wood at the corner of Middleton, and another on Lafayette Circle, the entire core of the community remained devoted to residences, churches, and schools.

Streetcar lines serving the suburbs of Cincinnati, 1880

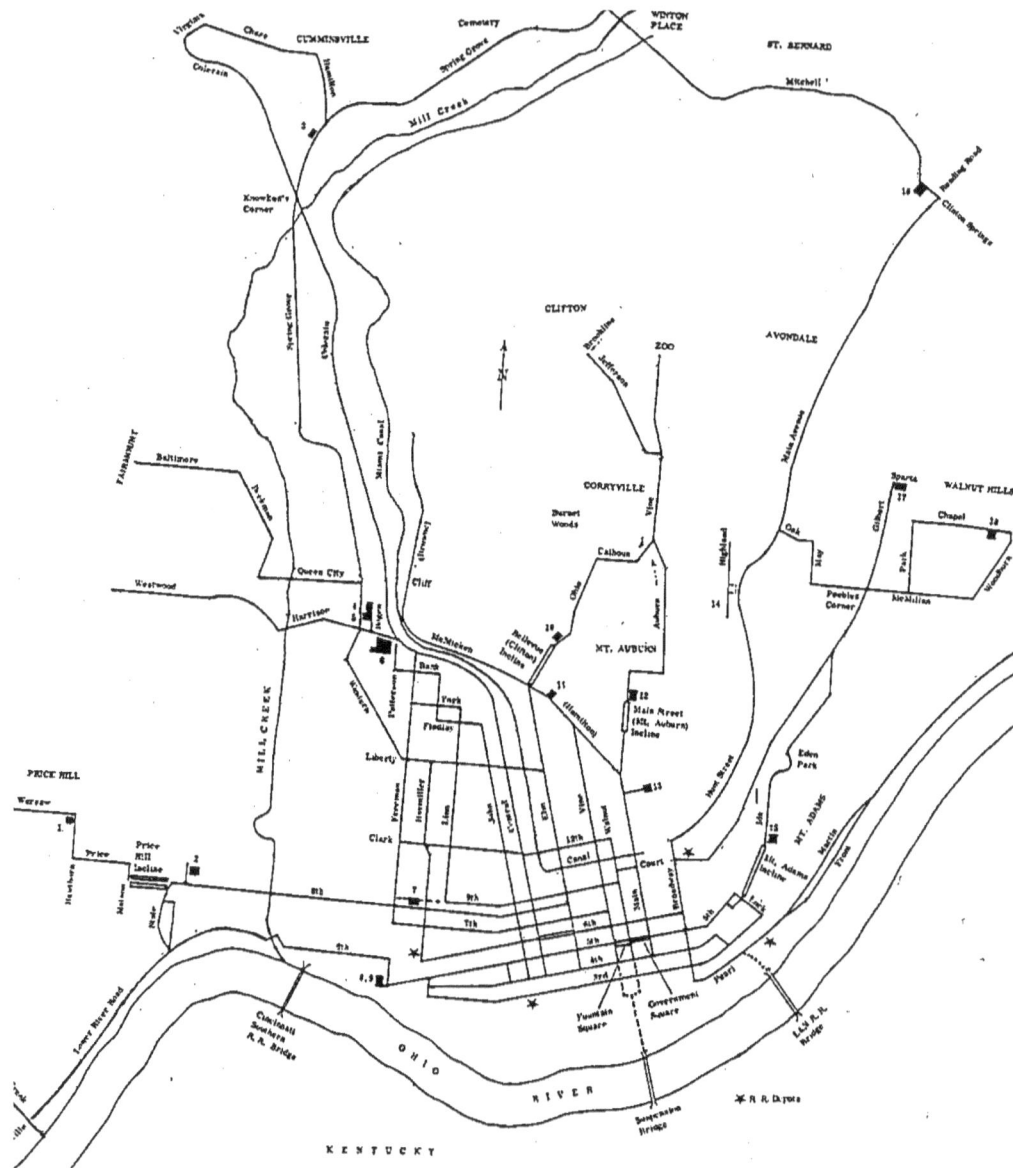

Clearly, annexation had not set Clifton off on a different angle of growth, nor had it destroyed the neighborhood's genteel ambiance. Indeed, in several respects affiliation with the city had improved the neighborhood. A new fire station, for example, had been constructed at the southwest corner of Clifton and Ludlow, where earlier the

Village's fire equipment had been kept in the center of the residential area, at Clifton and McAlpin. Equally important, action by the city helped establish a sharp boundary for the community on the west and at the same time prevented intensive development of that section. That end of Clifton, of course, still contained "The Windings'," occupied by the Sacred Heart Academy and the home of Mr. and Mrs. Max Fleischmann, a wedding gift presented to them by another of the "barons" of Lafayette Avenue, George K. Schoenberger. Next to the Fleischmann house, at the turn of the century, loomed Mt. Storm, a great white marble Italian Villa built in the mid 60s by Robert Bonner Bowler, an attorney, former mayor of Clifton, Democratic candidate for the 1st District Congressional seat, and Assistant Secretary of the Treasury of the United States under President Grover Cleveland. Bowler delighted in entertaining heads of state, especially royalty, and his gardener, Adolph Strauch, who designed the replica of Venus' Temple of Love which stands as the last vestige of the estate, formerly held the position of gardener for the Austrian Empire. After Bowler's unfortunate death in a runaway carriage accident on Sycamore Street, the city of Cincinnati purchased in 1911 the 66.74 acres of land from an heir for $115,270, a step which preserved the land from commercial or residential development and provided the west end of Clifton with a park to match Burnet Woods on its southeastern border.

Even Clifton School benefited from annexation. In 1905, a Cincinnati paper announced that "joy pervades the classic bailiwick of Clifton" because the Board of Education had accumulated enough money to finish the suburb's new elementary school. The effort began in 1903 when the President of the Board noted that "new buildings are very much needed in several parts of the city, notably in Clifton." By that time the suburb possessed more school age children than suitable school space, and the Board had erected barracks with a leaky, tar-paper roof for temporary accommodations. For that reason at least one resident, George R. Balch, boycotted the facilities by withholding his son from school. Between 1903 and 1905, however, the Board launched a major school construction program, and by June of 1905, the foundation for the Clifton building was in place. A delay which Superintendent of Schools F. B. Dyer characterized as an "unspeakable outrage" held up completion of the edifice for more than a year, but finally, after an

LUDLOW *business strip, as it appeared in 1922*

expenditure of $143,500 on the building and $3,692 for equipment, the school opened in the fall of 1906. It featured, as one reporter put it, "many things unknown to the other and last generation," including spacious corridors, a basement with lavatories, 14 classrooms, and an auditorium, a gymnasium, a library, and a restroom. Citizens of Clifton raised an additional $3,000 to embellish the interior of the building with statuary and pictures and to purchase library books. Everyone seemed pleased, and the Board of Education congratulated itself and the Cliftonites whose generosity adorned the building by noting that the new school had been visited by educators from other cities who pronounced it "the most beautiful in structure and equipment that they have seen."

CLIFTON AVENUE *as it appeared in 1898*

The other major change in Clifton's community structure during the 15 years after annexation had nothing to do with the city but reflected instead the movement of Catholicism to the hilltop suburbs. That process began in 1868 with the establishment of St. George's in Corryville (German), and proceeded with the appearance of St. Andrew's (Irish) in Avondale in 1874, and Holy Name (German and Irish) in Mt. Auburn in 1904. Clifton acquired its Catholic church, Annunciation, in 1910, an English-speaking parish served by Father James Kelly until 1944, as part of an effort to relieve the other hilltop parishes of the burden of serving the growing number of Catholics within their boundaries.

CHURCH OF THE ANNUNCIATION OF THE BLESSED VIRGIN MARY, *designed in the neoclassical style by Edward T. P. Graham. It was dedicated in 1930. Today the grounds are also home to Annunciation School.*

CLIFTON SCHOOL
Clifton and McAlpin Avenues, built 1905-06

Neighborhood and City

Clearly, then, Clifton experienced few essential changes in the 15 years following annexation. Since the 1880s it had became much more part of the city than before. Mass rapid transit provided close connections between it and the heart of the city and shifted its orientation, from Cumminsville to Fountain Square. Now it drew directly on the municipal corporation for parks, education, and fire and police protection, and it contributed taxes to the municipality in return for those and other services. In a fashion more direct and unmistakable than in the past, the fate of the city and the former suburb of Clifton seemed inextricably intertwined. Cliftonites, like others from similar neighborhoods, responded by seeking to control the fate of the city of which it was now irrevocably a part and with which its own future seemed so intimately connected. Urban politics now became a compelling interest of Clifton's civic minded citizens.

Cliftonites registered their views in city politics during the first quarter of the 20th century in essentially two ways. One was through participation in city-wide elections. In a manner familiar to readers of *Boss Cox's Cincinnati,* Cliftonites joined their fellow suburbanites in periodic efforts to purge the city of boss rule. In practical terms this meant that in every reform effort from 1897 through the adoption of the city-manager form of government in the mid-1920s, those who led the charge against control of the city and its schools by the dominant Republican machine found their staunchest supporters in peripheral neighborhoods like Clifton, Mt. Auburn, Avondale, Hyde Park, and Walnut Hills.

The anti-machine reformers also angled for political influence through another less familiar vehicle, the neighborhood improvement association. This movement began in the 1880s, in the wake of the great annexations after 1870 as an effort by outlying districts which felt underrepresented in a city council dominated by politicians from the smaller and more numerous wards nearer the heart of the city. Clifton joined the cause in 1896, the year of its annexation, when the Clifton and Burnet Woods Improvement Association adopted a constitution which stated the organization's objectives as "the advance of all modern improvements," such as the "opening of streets, extending rapid transit, beautifying, sprinkling and lighting of parks and avenues, improving walks, schools, etc." Yet this parochial spirit did not long rule the neighborhood associations. In 1907, the Clifton association and six others banded together to form the Federated Improvement Association. It was founded, according to one member, by some "of the widest awake and most self-sacrificing" citizens who wanted to "secure for themselves and for their children a larger control of every civic activity, so that this city shall become...a cleaner and more healthful and more beautiful place in which to live." The Reverend Charles Frederick Goss was impressed. "To attend a meeting of these delegates from associations representing every suburb and natural division of the city from Westwood to Madisonville and from the river to Wyoming is to be made profoundly certain that a civic consciousness of some kind is actually being born; that the soul of the city is awakening to new and nobler life....Today that comprehension is penetrating the minds of men, women, children and institutions in an amazing manner."

Others, apparently, agreed, for the Federation flourished. By 1913 it claimed some thirty-six constituent societies which represented 8,000 members. The public meeting was one of their favorite methods of advancing their cause. "Public opinion," claimed one Federationist, "moves the world," and "one of the best ways to mold a wise and enlightened opinion is by public meetings where men of all classes meet and discuss the needs of the people without political, religious or personal bias." Yet the city itself, as a kind of gigantic town meeting, was the best teacher. "Cities are playing a more and more important part in the life of the nation," he noted, and "in cities men have many interests in common to all, such as the use of streets, police, fire and health protection." There men "learn best how to work together, learn best the great truth that each must give up something for the good of all." In short, he concluded, "it is in cities that men, if given the chance of home rule, will learn most quickly the true foundation principles on which rest real freedom in a representative democracy."

Driven by this kind of confident optimism, and informed by an analysis of the city which stressed the interdependence of its elements, the Federation plunged enthusiastically into reform. It participated in the campaign for a sane Fourth of July to "increase the patriotism and decrease the casualties." It supported plans for a new trunk sewer system which would not only "redeem" the Mill Creek and reduce pollution in the city's water supply, but also develop "a revised standard of cleanliness and morality, a cleaner, healthier, and more progressive city. [It] means comfort, health and happiness, if you please, it may mean life itself." So the Federation urged the city to install "suitable, modern, sanitary drinking fountains" downtown, and decried the "common drinking cup" as a purveyor of tuberculosis, scarlet fever, diphtheria, measles, syphilis, infantile paralysis, and typhoid fever. The new fountains, reported a Federation committee, would help prevent "headaches, malaise and constipation" by making it easy for people in the center of the city, whether shoppers, residents, or workers, to get enough pure water.

The Federation also participated in the widespread efforts to reform the public schools characteristic of the teens. It took an active part in the drive for a small school board and in 1913 helped put up an independent ticket. It wanted school buildings used as social centers, arguing that they would develop a "wise, enlightened and progressive" public opinion by facilitating "free public discussion. Class distinctions, race and religious prejudices," claimed the Civic News, the organ of the Federation, "cannot live in the pure atmosphere of an open neighborhood meeting." The Federation also favored the teaching of sex hygiene in the schools because parents neglected the subject "by default" and, since sex was primarily a "technical matter," the church could be of little assistance.

Indeed, the Federation backed virtually every project for city improvement proposed during these years. It took part in a smoke abatement campaign and the "conservation movement" for fire prevention. It supported dairy inspection and urged the construction of better housing in the slums. It thought the abolition of gambling among children especially important lest there "raise up among us a race of gamblers and produce a condition worse than those which have been suppressed." Plans for the creation of more and better parks and playgrounds, the construction of a convention hall and an enlarged budget for the University of Cincinnati also received its endorsement.

The Federation felt it held a special relationship to local government. As President Starbuck Smith put it in 1912, "we are all busy men... trying to earn a living... and have felt compelled in the past to leave public affairs to the professional politician." But, he announced, "this organization…has proven that the time has come when the people of this city and county are going to take a real interest in and control of public affairs." More specifically, as the secretary of one of the affiliates put it, "what is demanded is a link connecting the citizen with City Hall, and the Improvement Association steps forward and provides the link," allowing "busy business men" who wanted to do more than just vote to participate in city affairs.

The Federation came up with several schemes to promote its concept of neighborhood democracy. It wanted to establish a municipal speakers' bureau to send lecturers to civic groups to keep them informed as to what the city planned to do. It endorsed the election of judges on a non-partisan ticket and urged jury reforms to eliminate compromise verdicts and mistrials and to prevent "the names of notorious cranks" from getting on the jury lists.

In 1912 and 1913 the Federation took an aggressive stand in the fight for a new city charter. It favored having a locally elected commission write the document because of "the great educational advantage it offers to all the citizens by their participation in formulating these changes and by the publicity which will be given the discussions of the city charter convention." It hoped the commissioners would adopt the federal system of government with a strong mayor, a small council elected at large, the non-partisan nomination and election of all municipal officers, a short ballot, and an extended civil service system. The Federation trusted, too, that "other such simplifications of the machinery of government as will tend to make it more efficient and responsive to the city's needs"

including that "powerful trinity of democracy," the initiative, referendum, and recall, would be written into the charter.

Some Federationists wanted to carry democracy farther than this.

> MILL CREEK *is a 24-mile stream emptying into the Ohio River at Cincinnati. It powered early mills, served as a canal route, and in the early 20th century, functioned as a sewer for neighboring communities. Today, a million people live in its 166 square mile watershed, and it has benefited from active conservation by volunteer groups.*

Charles Sawyer, a young lawyer from Hyde Park, thought the charter should provide not only "strict regulation" for public utilities, but also for a "gigantic" municipal heat, light, and power plant. Nor was that all. He asked for the establishment of a central municipal market, a city-owned central depot and interurban terminal, "model" city tenements, a new municipal court for civil and criminal cases, free legal services for the poor, a department of accounting, and "a special body for urban planning."

This kind of charter, Sawyer claimed, was not justified by the erroneous American idea "that we can cure all our political diseases by a clever manipulation of the forms of government." The valid rationale for innovation lay elsewhere. "The only real and permanent improvements," Sawyer contended, "come through an aroused interest, a wider knowledge and a broader point of view on the part of the every-day citizen. For this reason the chief value of many suggested changes in the machinery of government, both local and national, is educational."

By the late 1920s much of the program of suburban municipal reformers had become reality. By then a city manager and a small council elected at large by proportional representation comprised the municipal government, and that government possessed a planning commission, which defined the city as a large community of interdependence, the product of the interaction of smaller communities, as a key agency in coordinating the development of the whole. Throughout the early 1920s the commission worked on such a plan, and in 1925, just before the revolution in local government which brought a new charter and a new party to power in Cincinnati, the *Official Plan of the City of Cincinnati* was adopted. This was the first comprehensive plan adopted by a city the size of the Queen City, and although it contains no section on neighborhoods as such, an implicit concern for these entities permeated the document and reflected the dominant concerns of reformers from suburban districts like Clifton, as well as of the new professional urbanists who formulated municipal policy.

Apart from anxiety over the city's continuing low rate of population increase expressed in Chapter I, the Plan's chief explicit preoccupation was with what we would call improving the quality of life. The principal instrument for attaining that goal, according to the Plan, was zoning, a new legal mechanism designed to secure the integrity of neighborhoods. In a section entitled "The Need for Zoning," it noted that a survey indicated that "hundreds of stores, public-garages and even industrial plants had invaded home neighborhoods. Each case was tending to lower neighboring real estate values, with a corresponding loss to the city in ratables [taxes, and therefore services]." Elsewhere a "number of apartment houses were invading open detached home districts, hundreds of buildings were found to blanket their neighbors by projecting well in front of them," and "garages and billboards were located anywhere, regardless of their effect on neighboring property."

Such conditions threatened even the most affluent sections in a city made up of neighborhoods which, like Clifton, might possess a purely residential core but found it circumscribed by a periphery of mixed land uses. The problem was how to assert control by the city so it could determine "in black and white...just what could and could not be done on every lot in the whole 72 square miles of the city." The answer seemed to be zoning carried out as an integral part of "the rest of the City Plan, for all the parts of the plan are inter-related. Thoroughfares determine the location of future business, industrial and apartment house districts. They control the bus lines, present and proposed, and fix the location of business and apartment houses. The type of subdivision layout controls the types of residences. Parkways attract apartment houses, especially near the center of the city. Schools and playgrounds should be surrounded by residence districts, as should also parks and play fields. In general, it was found that unless the zoning plan is studied jointly with the rest of the City Plan, it would be likely to be' just a good guess and continuance of existing conditions, rather than a creative force for the logical and orderly development of the growing city."

Such a conception of the city rested on the assumption of continuous, albeit in Cincinnati's case, modest growth, and that meant inevitable neighborhood change. The section of the Plan on subdivisions and housing took up this question in general and as it might affect Clifton in particular. Its language suggested that the planners saw no immediate threat to Clifton or similar neighborhoods. Almost nonchalantly the plan predicted that the "highest cost and most open type of housing, such as is found today in the Grandin Road district, and in Clifton, will always be limited in quantity and in a sense, can look out for itself," In fact, the document found "considerable room for expansion of the same type in Clifton and to a lesser extent, in Avondale." Over the long haul, this segment of the Plan concluded, "all this should be encouraged," but added casually, almost as an after thought, that "it is obvious from the history of other cities that the older developments nearer in, will gradually give place to a more intensive development and the best type of housing will gradually move farther out." Peering into that future the planners proposed to encourage the location of "the best type of housing" in Indian Hill, and in sparsely settled areas north and west of Wyoming, north and west of Mt. Airy Forest, and along the heights back from the river in Delhi, southwest of Price Hill.

The chance of having to move to those places must have seemed remote to Cliftonites in the 1920s. Had they not, through their enlightened participation in municipal politics and the unselfish activities of their neighborhood association helped endow the city with the most efficient, businesslike government yet devised in America? And could they not, through their influence in civic affairs, defend Clifton's interests while assisting in the noble task of guiding public policy along a path which coordinated and controlled neighborhood growth in such a manner as to foster the balanced and healthy growth of that larger organic community .of which Clifton itself was such an important part? To those in the 1920s who rode along the broad, cool expanse of Clifton Avenue, strolled or skated in Burnet Woods at the edge of the neighborhood, sipped a soda in the Busy Bee delicatessen or shopped for hardware in the Ludlow business strip, Clifton must have seemed, indeed, quite able to take care of itself.

For almost three decades it was, but by the 1940s the sorts of changes which frightened and inspired the Clifton anti-annexationists of 1896 had begun to set in. Clifton's population reached 9,800 in 1940, and rose sharply over the next five years as a consequence of increased apartment construction. Between 1940 and 1945 a total of 220 dwelling units were built in Clifton, but only 60 were single family houses. Of the rest, 24 housed two to three families, 88 accommodated 4 families, and 48 contained five to nine families. Even so the situation seemed far from critical, at least to the planners who prepared the residential areas study for the metropolitan master plan of 1948, for they chose "protection" rather than "rehabilitation," "conservation," or "preparation for growth" as the appropriate "treatment" for the neighborhood. The master plan itself suggested only minor modifications in and immediately around Clifton, most of them related to traffic control, and it described Clifton as an area with "many single-family high-cost residences and many fine old mansions," added that "some of the original estate tracts have been sub-divided and expensive new residences erected," and noted without comment the cluster of "large apartments" near the business center at Ludlow and Clifton Avenue.

BURNET WOODS, *ca. 1902*

Neighborhood as City: The Rise of the Community in Clifton

These observations aid recommendations seemed innocuous and familiar enough, but the Metropolitan Master Plan, published in 1948, should have caused more concern. Couched in soberly reassuring and undramatic terms, the plan departed radically from the 1925 comprehensive plan's conception of the city as a larger organic community composed of interdependent and inseparable neighborhoods. The 1948 scheme instead rested upon the assumption that the city no longer constituted a viable social unit. This notion, the plan explained,, "is based on the observation that when a city expands beyond a certain size it reaches the point of diminishing returns in terms of advantages which a city, as a social community, should provide for its inhabitants. Somewhere in the course of its growth a city attains the optimum stage with reference to the conveniences of living or the economy of public and private services. When the metropolitan city grows beyond this size there is a progressive multiplication of problems, complexities and inconveniences and of the costs of operation and waste of time, money and human effort."

From that point the logic led directly to the abandonment of the idea of "natural" neighborhoods, which had been so "given" in the 1925 plan that its authors 'took it for granted and felt no need to discuss it as a separate subject, but blithely prescribed zoning as the sovereign remedy for minor defects in the expected course of urban growth. In 1925, community at the city-wide level would be produced out of the interaction of neighborhood cells.

The 1948 plan moved from a different diagnosis to a different prognosis. It proposed to "reintroduce in Cincinnati as a metropolitan center the advantages of the self-contained city of medium size." The plan conceived of these "communities" as "cities of about 20,000 to 40,000 population, self-contained in respect to the everyday life of their inhabitants except for such facilities and services as will ' continue to be located in or supplied by Cincinnati as the central city, and by institutions serving the Metropolitan Area."

The conception of a metropolitan area composed of a central city, which existed exclusively for and as a governing body, and of clusters of medium-sized cities, some inside and some outside the jurisdiction of the major municipality in the area, and with no more vital connection to it than sheer convenience, left no space for "neighborhoods" like Clifton. The plan of 1948 tried to break the news gently, but its meaning was clearly stated. The old neighborhoods were to be phased out and replaced by new and larger communities. "Fortunately," the plan noted, a basis already "existed for "organizing" the metropolitan area into what it called "communities and neighborhoods." The Cincinnati metropolitan area in fact was composed "of any number of natural residential communities with separate identities as social and civic units. Building on this foundation the Master Plan rounds out the system and reinforces it by introducing features that will maintain and strengthen the unity of these communities of 20,000 to 40,000 people. The physical plan cannot, of course, create a community or a neighborhood but it can and will assist other forces in fostering a true community and neighborhood spirit."

The plan cited four basic factors critical to the viability of the new communities which it proposed to create or acknowledge. Each should be served by a junior high school and a cluster of feeder elementary schools. Each should possess a "community business district, a secondary business district in relation to the Metropolitan Area as a whole, but the chief center of commercial activities so far as the community is concerned." Each should contain a community civic center near the business center composed of a branch library, a recreation center, a health center, a branch post office, and in some cases appropriate semi-public buildings. Last, the boundaries of each community should be drawn with reference to "separators," such as topographic features, industrial belts, railroads, expressways, large parks, greenbelts, and cemeteries and institutions.

This new vision of the city placed the old "neighborhood" of Clifton in the new "community" of Clifton Hills, an entity composed officially of an amalgamation of Camp Washington, Clifton, Corryville, Mt. Auburn, and University Heights. More important, perhaps, the proposal to organize the life of the area around centralized facilities within the community not only left little in the way of significant functions for the old "neighborhoods," but also implied that residents of the communities should concern themselves with provincial affairs and leave city-wide and metropolitan concerns to others.

While the details and implications of the new-communities idea may have proved disquieting to those Cliftonites who still regarded the relationship between neighborhood and city as natural, symbiotic, and stimulating, two other aspects of the plan deserved equal attention. The first referred to the traditional concern with separating commercial, industrial, and residential districts. That view appeared in the 1925 plan, but in 1948, the distinction between "areas for living" and "areas in which to make a living" was drawn more sharply than in 1925. Nor did the planners of 1948 rely exclusively on zoning to promote the desired segregation of land-use patterns. Instead, they contended that deteriorated residential neighborhoods polluted by too much industry should be destroyed and turned over to commercial or industrial uses. Most of those neighborhoods lay in valleys, the most important of which, from Clifton's vantage point, was the valley of the Mill Creek.

The other aspect of the plan which Cliftonites might have viewed with anxiety dealt with transportation. The section of the plan on that subject 'noted that the Federal Interregional Highway Plan (1944) laid out a national network of freeways and expressways designed primarily to connect the principal cities of the country and to relieve traffic congestion in urban areas. Three links in the system came through Cincinnati: U.S. 25 from Detroit via Cincinnati to Atlanta and Florida; an unnumbered route from Cleveland by way of Cincinnati to the Gulf States; and U.S. 52 from Cincinnati to Indianapolis. The 1948 master plan sought to accommodate these highways and laid down guidelines for their location. It suggested, specifically, routing them so as to drain heavy traffic movements from overloaded thoroughfares, to serve concentrations of industrial and commercial activities, and to assure that the benefits they provided would not sacrifice maximum efficiency or desirable community development. On this last point the plan added that where alternatives existed routes "should be favored which will remove from the tax duplicate the least amount of valuable property, fit in best with the land use, and not involve unjustifiable cost for construction. "

Translated onto the map, that recommendation, plus the plans for sharply differentiating industrial from residential areas, meant that Mill Creek Valley, which housed both industry and, in its lower reaches, the bulk of Cincinnati's poor and over half of its black population, would be the site of massive redevelopment and highway construction projects, provided that Congress, the state, and other political bodies took the necessary steps after the War. It also set some planners and city officials to thinking about where in the metropolitan area the population uprooted by urban redevelopment and expressway construction might resettle.

In the years just after World War II, while the master plan of 1948 remained merely a paper prospectus, Cincinnati's communities and neighborhoods changed slowly. During the 1950s, however, a combination of federal, state, county, and city activity placed much of its urban redevelopment and expressway program in motion. By the late 1950s, I-75 and the Queensgate I and Laurel-Richmond homes projects in the Mill Creek Valley and the West End were underway. Each month 210 families fled the path of the Mill Creek Expressway, and one agency estimated that 10,000 families left the Queensgate I area before its completion. Some doubtless left the metropolitan area, but the others, coupled with newcomers from the South, sought out new homes within the city. The shift of population set off reactions in other communities which suggested, conventional wisdom to the contrary notwithstanding, that the city still functioned very much like an organic system of interdependent elements.

Walnut Hills felt the trauma first. Since the mid-19th century a small but growing enclave of black families lived in that neighborhood, and by 1940 the census listed a total of 2,595 non-white families there. Demolition of much of the West End and Mill Creek Valley districts, however, set off a black migration which hit Walnut Hills first, then pressed westward into Mt. Auburn, Corryville, and through the lower part of Avondale to the north until it washed over the bottom edge of Clifton's eastern slope along Vine Street. There, in the mid-1970s, it stopped. But before then, as the new black ghetto took shape, it displaced lower-middle, middle, and upper-middle class whites and produced an angry white backlash on the one hand and, on the other, an outburst of violence by blacks infuriated by their removal from the

West End and frustrated and embittered at their re-imprisonment in yet another ghetto. The era of the long hot summer and the neighborhood organization revolution had reached Cincinnati and Clifton.

The years between 1950 and 1970, then, marked another critical period in Clifton's history and a revival of the sense, among some at least, that its essence might once more be violated. The outcome is not yet clear. In this period, the gradual implementation of the 1948 master plan's "new community" program, combined with the ramifications of urban redevelopment and expressway construction in Cincinnati more generally, posed an unprecedented challenge to the traditional structure, role, and function of Clifton as a neighborhood since the late 19th century. The expansion of research and higher education facilities in the "greater Clifton" area during the 1950s and 1960s proved both helpful in meeting that challenge, in the sense that they attracted middle-income and highly educated families to the area, and hurtful in the sense that their arrival created a fissure between "old" and "new" residents on both sides of Ludlow Avenue. The appearance of new people in historic Clifton, for example, made the area predominantly but not overwhelmingly Democratic in national politics, and "liberal" on social issues, a prospect which displeased some old Cliftonites, but which in any case provided the backdrop for the emergence of local controversy about membership policies in the Clifton Meadows Swim (and now Tennis) Club, the role of semi-public organizations in the development of housing policies for Clifton, and as abundant gossip about the night-spots in the Ludlow Avenue business strip and the programs held at St. Johns Unitarian Church.

The elements and the configurations of these changes of the 1950s and 60s made Clifton a lively, stimulating, and urbane in which to live, at least by Cincinnati standards. But they also help to explain the flourishing state of such voluntaristic organizations as Clifton Town Meeting, established in 1962, and the emergence of an energetic and imaginative cadre of parents who became increasingly involved with the future of Clifton School, and then with city-wide school matters, during the late 1960s and early 70s. In addition, this perspective on the contemporary crisis of neighborhood and city helps explain the paradox of the 1975 *Clifton Community Plan*.

A product of the joint efforts of Clifton Town Meeting, the Cincinnati

City Planning Commission, and student consultants from the Graduate Department of Community Planning at the University of Cincinnati, the *Clifton Community Plan* asserts Clifton's uniqueness and right of self-determination in a way which suggests uneasiness about (but not quite repudiation of) the definition of community for Clifton which emerged from the 1948 master plan and from city policies carried out subsequently in its spirit. This definition merged Clifton's fate with the fate of Camp Washington, Corryville, Mount Auburn, and University Heights, and against this, the *Clifton Community Plan* projects an image of Clifton as a bucolic and isolated 19th century village, with a present continuous with its past. At the same time, it recognizes the importance to modern Clifton and modern Cliftonites, and hence it seeks to retain in the Clifton environs a variety of research and educational institutions, and to develop educational and recreational facilities cut in a sophisticated cosmopolitan, and decidedly contemporary mold. To do this, it presents a truncated account of Clifton's history, which measures the present against the presumably serene past of an allegedly autonomous place—a past which ended abruptly with annexation in 1896. Then, without a word of explanation for the missing 80 years, the Plan projects an optimistic view of Clifton's future as part of a city and metropolis whose history, current status, and future prospects it blithely ignores.

Clifton at the opening of the last quarter of the 20th century seemed tempted, this analysis suggests, to turn inward and backward, to assume that Clifton somehow could take care of itself, and to forget its potential role as a dynamic place both in and of the city and metropolis of which it remained irrevocably a part. Indeed, nothing illustrates more strikingly the lure of parochialism in the contemporary neighborhood-organization enthusiasm than the contrast between the "provincial" constitution adopted by the Clifton and Burnet Woods Improvement association in 1896 and the *Clifton Community Plan* of 1975. The former was soon abandoned in the belief that only the redemption of the city could save the neighborhoods, the latter stands curiously silent on this very issue, the question of the relationship of neighborhood and community to city and metropolis.

Yet the "provincialism" of the 1975 Plan was not the product of narrow minded neighborhood chauvinists. Its creators and promulgators were precisely those persons with the broadest and most cosmopolitan view of the role of Clifton in Cincinnati and of Cincinnati in the metropolitan area. Of necessity, however, theirs was a view without clear focus. In the absence of such confident notions of the nature and function of suburbs, neighborhoods, and communities as characterized the earlier 20th century, indeed, our characteristic contemporary response has emerged increasingly as a retreat to a past which seems certain, a past which seems to provide at once a base on which to build a conception of community growth and development and a standard against which to measure the present. Yet to their great credit, Clifton and Cliftonites in the 1970s seemed unwilling to act decisively on that characteristic contemporary impulse to find in the mythic history of Clifton Village as a separate place before annexation a design for the present and the future, perhaps because they, like those first residents of Clifton in the 1840s, knew at first hand the delights as well as the dilemma of being in, but not of the city.

Further Reading

Clubbe, John. *Cincinnati Observed: Architecture and History*. Columbus: Ohio State University Press, 1992.
> A guide to the city by a non-resident and urbane admirer of the Queen City which contains an insightful and at times biting section about Clifton written from an angle different from that in this booklet.

Fairbanks, Robert B. and Patricia Mooney-Melvin, Editors. *Making Sense of the City: Local Government, Civic Culture, and Community Life in Urban America*. Columbus: Ohio State University Press, 2001.
> Essays by "Cincinnati school" urban historians which provide quick and handy illustrations of the versatility of that approach. Most of the chapters deal with aspects of the history of Cincinnati and its neighborhoods and suburbs.

Miller, Zane L. and Bruce Tucker. *Changing Plans For America's Inner Cities: Cincinnati's Over the Rhine and Twentieth Century Urbanism*. Columbus: Ohio State University Press, 1998.
> A history of one of Cincinnati's most famous and notorious neighborhoods, the development of which coincided chronologically with that of Clifton and the history of which, perhaps surprisingly, will sound familiar to readers of the Shapiro/Miller brief history of Clifton.

Miller, Zane L. *Boss Cox's Cincinnati: Urban Politics in the Progressive Era*. New York: Oxford University Press, 1968.
> A study of the famous power broker and Clifton resident who facilitated Clifton's annexation and who outraged Cincinnati reform politicians and civic leaders, including many residents of Clifton.

———. *Suburb: Neighborhood and Community in Forest Park, Ohio, 1935-1976*. Knoxville: University of Tennessee Press, 1981.
> This study demonstrates that trends, tendencies, issues, and problems in urban politics characteristic of Clifton's development also played themselves out in the building and development of this planned suburb and American generally.

———. *Visions of Place: The City, Neighborhoods, Suburbs, and Cincinnati's Clifton, 1850-2000.* Columbus: Ohio State University Press, 2001.
 Visions of Place not only provides a comprehensive history of Clifton from its origins into the last decades of the twentieth century, it also contains in an Appendix a concise statement of the fundamental elements of the "Cincinnati school" approach to doing history as construed by Miller.

Painter, Sue Ann. *Architecture in Cincinnati: An Illustrated History of Designing and Building an American City.* Athens: Ohio University Press, 2006.
 A lavishly illustrated (352 pages of images) examination of the city's built environment, chronologically organized, featuring commentary by Jayne Merkel, an important architectural historian and a former Cincinnati Enquirer architecture critic, and by Beth Sullebarger, an historic preservation expert who served for seveal years on the staff of Cinicnnati's Historic Conservation Office. Clifton receives its share of their attention.

Shapiro, Henry D. and and Jonathan Sarna, editors. *Ethnic Diversity and Civic Identity: Patterns of Conflict and Cohesion in Cincinnati since 1820.* Urbana: University of Illinois Press, 1992.
 A collection of essays that explores themes examined in the Clifton booklet but from a different point of view. Shapiro's introduction draws on the mode of thought he brought to the Laboratory in American Civilization.

———. *Appalachia on Our Mind: The Southern Mountains and Mountaineers in the American Consciousness, 1870-1920.* Chapel Hill: University of North Carolina Press, 1978.
 Many Cincinnati school members regard this as Shapiro's magnum opus. It does not deal directly with Clifton, or Cincinnati, but it offers a prime example of "symptomatic" history, ways in which it may be used to illustrate concepts of culture and place in the late 19th and early twentieth century and how they influenced changing views of regionalism and urbanism, including the handling of ethnic, religious, class, and racial diversity at the metropolitan scale.

About the Authors

ZANE L. MILLER grew up in Lima, Ohio, and Peru, Indiana, and earned an M.A. at Miami University, Ohio, and a Ph.D. at the University of Chicago, where he served as a research assistant to Bessie Louise Pierce, the author of a three volume history of Chicago, and specialized in urban history under the supervision of Richard C. Wade, for whom he wrote a dissertation (1966) that became *Boss Cox's Cincinnati: Urban Politics in the Progressive Era*, published originally by Oxford University Press (1968). After teaching a year at Northwestern University, he came to the University of Cincinnati where he taught for over thirty years. Over the course of his career, he collaborated extensively with Henry Shapiro. He is the author of many essays, articles, reviews, and books. He also supervised a number of master's theses and doctoral dissertation, helping prepare a number of students for successful careers as historians. He retired from teaching, but not scholarship in 1999. He is now Charles Phelps Taft Professor of History Emeritus at the University of Cincinnati, and serves as senior co-editor of the Urban Life, Landscape and Policy Series (ten volumes in print to date) for Temple University Press.

Charles F. Casey-Leininger
University of Cincinnati

HENRY D. SHAPIRO was born in New York City in 1937 and raised there. He earned his M.A. at Cornell and his Ph.D. at Rutgers. Shapiro's Cornell M.A. Thesis, "Confiscation of Confederate Property in the North," (1961) was published by that university's press in 1962. At Rutgers, Shapiro specialized in intellectual history under the supervision of Warren Susman for whom he wrote a dissertation (1966) that would become his seminal *Appalachia on Our Mind: The Southern Mountains and Mountaineers in the American Consciousness, 1870-1920* (1978).

In 1966, Henry Shapiro received his Ph.D. and accepted an offer to teach American intellectual history and the history of science at the University of Cincinnati. He quickly discovered in the life of the physician-naturalist-entrepreneur-city booster Daniel Drake an apt means to combine his two passions. More importantly, he met his lifelong intellectual sidekick, collaborator and friend, Zane L. Miller. Together these young Turks set out to refashion the university and to open new historical vistas. Drake, reputed founder of the university, became the touchstone for encouraging the university to preserve and explore its history. Shapiro directed the new medical history archives and labored to get Cincinnati to hire a medical historian. He also developed collections for other parts of the university's past, such as the Ohio Mechanics Institute.

The mercurial Shapiro provided much of the intellectual basis, while Miller masterfully worked out implications as well as sharpened insights. Their collaboration first resulted in the co-edited *Daniel Drake: Physician to the West* (1971). In this and other efforts, method dominated their discussions. Shapiro was smitten with French structuralism from Levi-Strauss to Foucault, who showed that it was human to taxonimize reality. Shapiro concluded that what held together human societies at various times and places was sharing similar taxonomies. It was in the context of those shared taxonomies that public action took place.

This exciting revelation focused attention directly on cultural ideas. It was cultural ideas—taxonomies of reality perceived in a particular way—that both "caused" conditions and situations, some of which may have been longstanding, to become seen as problems that demanded amelioration as well as circumscribed the arena and methods by which amelioration could successfully occur. Among other things, that understanding posited race, gender, class, religion and the rest not as universal social forces or constructs but rather products of culture. And like cultures themselves, these products were temporal, the product of certain specific taxonomies.

To Shapiro, the use of culture in this manner rescued intellectual history from its malaise. It accentuated the ideas themselves, not the cultural-social demographics of their genesis. After a year at Harvard's Charles Warren Center, Shapiro and Miller created the Laboratory in American Civilization. Patterned in spirit after the Chicago School of Sociology's "the City as Laboratory," the Shapiro/Miller effort took Cincinnati as its locus only because they were there. Events in Cincinnati were "symptomatic"—indicative but neither identical nor extraordinary—of what happened elsewhere in America at the similar time. Undergraduates learned about history by doing history. Working with graduate students, each did original research on some relatively minor act at a certain time in Cincinnati. Later lab discussions put those apparently discrete acts together--why those events or acts were done in that way at that time and how they might have changed at later times. *Clifton: Neighborhood and Community in an Urban Setting* (1976) became the first lab product.

Shapiro's insistence on culture as a central project in intellectual history emphasized place and the bonds that categorized it. But he recognized that interpretation of place was itself a cultural construct. He was fascinated by the idea of place, the idea of regionalism and regional identity and the idea of otherness rather than the fact of those designations. Nowhere was this truer than in his seminal *Appalachia on Our Mind*, which was published as Shapiro filled a Fulbright scholarship in Berlin. Started as his dissertation 15 years earlier, Shapiro began with this caveat, "This is not a history of Appalachia. It is a history of the idea of Appalachia, and therefore the invention of Appalachia." Here the analysis focuses on how Appalachia emerged as a strange land and peculiar people and how Americans using that construct acted through it in an effort to
understand American civilization.

Ironically, Shapiro emerged as a major figure among scholars of Appalachia as identity politics took charge. Always nattily attired in a three-piece wool suit and blue oxford cloth shirt no matter the season, the full-bearded Shapiro sat on the board of Appalachian Journal, wrote introductions to various collections and volumes and reviewed countless others. His *Appalachia on Our Mind* remains in print some 26 years after its initial publication.

Fascination with the idea of place dominated Shapiro's thinking as he continued his fruitful collaboration with Miller. Together they formed the University of Cincinnati's Center for Neighborhood and Community Studies and edited the Urban Life and Landscape series for Ohio State University Press. Forty titles have been published there.

Alan I. Marcus
Mississippi State University

www.ingramcontent.com/pod-product-compliance
Lightning Source LLC
Chambersburg PA
CBHW030455010526
44118CB00011B/949